夏宫论坛

SUMMER PALACE FORUM

第二辑

中国·国际关系学院

·北京·

图书在版编目（CIP）数据

夏宫论坛：国际组织人才培养与发展 / 国际关系学院编.
北京：中国经济出版社，2017.9
ISBN 978-7-5136-4439-6

Ⅰ.①夏… Ⅱ.①国… Ⅲ.①国际组织—人才培养—文集 Ⅳ.①D813-53 ②C961-53

中国版本图书馆 CIP 数据核字（2016）第 260303 号

策划编辑　伏建全
责任编辑　孙晓霞
文字编辑　孙喆浩
责任印制　马小宾
封面设计　任燕飞

出版发行　中国经济出版社
印 刷 者　北京金明盛印刷有限公司
经 销 者　各地新华书店
开　　本　787mm×1092mm　1/16
印　　张　10
字　　数　200 千字
版　　次　2017 年 9 月第 1 版
印　　次　2017 年 9 月第 1 次印刷
定　　价　98.00 元
广告经营许可证　京西工商广字第 8179 号

中国经济出版社 **网址** www.economyph.com **社址** 北京市西城区百万庄北街 3 号 **邮编** 100037

目　录

CHAPTER 1

刘　慧

国际关系学院校党委书记

国际战略与安全研究中心主任

Liu Hui, Party Secretary of UIR; Director of CISSS

第二届夏宫论坛致辞

尊敬的玛丽埃塔学院布鲁诺校长，尊敬的对外经济贸易大学王玲书记，尊敬的各位来宾，各位老师、同学，大家上午好！

首先，我代表国际关系学院对第二届夏宫论坛的召开表示热烈祝贺！对来自美国、德国、日本、中国澳门和国内的嘉宾，表示诚挚欢迎和衷心感谢！

两年前，即2013年6月，美国玛丽埃塔学院与中国国际关系学院共同创办了首届夏宫论坛，论坛的主题是“高等院校的社会责任及与企（商）业界的关系”。在两天时间里，美国著名大学和国内知名大学的学者以及企业界人士，围绕“高校·创新·合作”的主题开展了广泛、新颖而富有探索精神的国际研讨。

论坛场面十分活跃，气氛热烈，至今历历在目。与会专家学者一致感到，合作激发创新，合作与创新带来力量和福利。高校的学者和学生一方面是跨国合作的受益者，同时也是合作的推动者。在全球合作发展中，高校是重要的先锋和力量。因此，高等院校应当在自身发展中，更多地承担社会和世界的责任，为全世界的合作和创新贡献我们知识分子的聪明和智慧，贡献我们的爱心和力量。

本届论坛在首届论坛的基础上，将“创新教育，创造价值，服务社会——

国际组织人才培养与发展”作为主题。如果说首届论坛的核心关键词是“责任”,那么,此次论坛的关键词就是“创造”。在今年“两会”上,“创客”等网络热词写进李克强总理的政府工作报告,从一个角度证明了当今中国正在发生着什么,改变着什么。在我国经济全面转型升级中,大众的思维模式在发生变化,年轻人赶超前辈的创新意识在增强,更愿意将梦想和创意变成现实。由此,“MAKER”“创客”在中国语境里,被赋予开拓梦想、实现梦想的含义。而实现梦想、成就创新,需要我们有更加开放的世界和更加包容的社会。高校应做什么?高校能做什么?我想,这是我们广泛邀请各国、各方面专家进行深入研讨的目的。

我要特别感谢我们的合作伙伴——美国玛丽埃塔学院和他的团队的支持。

去年,布鲁诺校长来我校一起庆祝两校建立合作关系20周年。21年中,玛校在提供学生奖学金和教师进修方面做出了极大的贡献,两校开辟了学生交流、教师交流、干部和管理人员交流,双方师生建立了深厚的友谊。借此机会,我代表全校师生向布鲁诺校长和玛丽埃塔学院的各位领导、教授表示衷心的感谢!

我国党和国家最高领导人习近平说:中国要永远做一个学习大国。一个国家对外开放,必须首先推进人的对外开放,特别是人才的对外开放。如果人思想禁锢、心胸封闭,那就不可能有真正的对外开放。因此,对外开放要着眼于人、着力于人,推动人们在眼界上、思想上、知识上、技术上走向开放。面对国际形势飞速变革,我国政府大力推动开放创新,采取的一系列政策都贯穿着改革创新的理念和精神。高校的责任是努力造就一批创新型、外向型人才,为国家实施创新驱动发展战略,以及为中国在国际舞台上发挥重要作用提供雄厚的后备力量。

国际关系学院一直致力于培养具有精湛的外语能力、开阔的国际视野和扎实的基础知识的人才,在本科生和研究生教育中积极倡导创新型和外向型人才培养模式:一是专业和课程设置以“国际”为核心,训练学生的国际战略思维;二是在多个学科建立校企合作实践基地,提高学生实践能力和综合素质;三是为学术项目和创业项目提供支持,培养学生研究和解决实际问题的能力;四是长期专注于国际热点问题研究,取得了一系列重要成果。

人才战略的核心是培养。今天,我们齐聚国际关系学院探讨关于创新教育和国际组织人才培养的问题。我们真诚希望各位与会人员畅所欲言、各抒己见,共同探索创新教育和人才培养之路,为全球繁荣、人类文明做出努力和贡献。

预祝论坛圆满成功!

Address at the 2nd Summer Palace Forum

Honorable President of Marietta College Mr. Bruno, Party Secretary of "University of International Business and Economics" Wang Ling, Distinguished guests, Dear teachers and students, Good morning!

At the outset, on behalf of the University of International Relations, I wish to extend warm congratulations on the opening of the second Summer Palace Forum. I also take this opportunity to extend our sincere welcome and heartfelt thanks to the guests from the United States, Germany, Japan, Macao and mainland China.

Two years ago, in June 2013, Marietta College from the U. S. and the University of International Relations of China co-founded the first Summer Palace Forum, aiming at the theme of "Higher Educations' Social Responsibilities & Its Relations with Society Business Community". Within two days, scholars from American and domestic famous universities, together with businessmen, conducted extensive discussions with innovative and exploratory spirits around the topic of "Campus · Creativity · Cooperation". The scene of the forum's lively atmosphere is still vivid in my mind. Scholars and experts at the forum all agreed that cooperation and innovation yields creativity, strength , and various benefits. As beneficiaries of transnational cooperation, scholars and students from campus also play the role of facilitator for cooperation. Besides, the global cooperation and development has witnessed higher education as an important pioneer and force. Consequently, higher education should shoulder more responsibility for society and the world, contribute more smartness and wisdom of intellectuals, devote love, as well as energy for the worldwide cooperation and innovation within its self-development.

On the basis of the first Summer Palace Forum, the theme of this year's forum is "Serving Society through Innovative Education and Creative Value——Talent Cultivation and Development for International Organizations". Different from "responsibility", the key word for the first forum, this forum adopts "Creativity" instead. The emergence of network hot words, such as "Maker"(创客), in Premier Li's Government Work Report in the Two Sessions of this year, has proved from one perspective that China today is undergoing changes. In other words, in the period of completely transitional and upgrade of China's economy, people's thinking patterns are changing in a way that young people prefer to turn their dreams and creativities into reality with a stonger innovative awareness outpacing predecessors. Therefore, the word "Maker" is given a new meaning of exploring and realizing one's dream in the context of Chinese language. While a more open world and a more inclusive society are what we need to fulfill our dreams and maintain innovations. In response, what should campuses do and what we can do? I believe that this is why we invite experts of various aspects from countries to carry out an in-depth discussion on these issues.

I would like to express my particular thanks to our cooperative partner——Marietta College and its team for their great support. Last year, President Bruno came and joined the celebration the 20th anniversary of establishing cooperative relation between our two schools. The last 21 years have also witnessed the tremendous contribution made by your side in terms of providing scholarship for students and training for teachers. In addition, both sides have created channels for students, teachers, cadres, and administrative staff to exchange views, contributing to a deep friendship among students and teachers. Again, on behalf of our faculty and students, let me take this opportunity to express heartfelt thanks to the President Bruno , officials and professors of Marietta College.

According to President Xi Jinping, the top party and state leader, China shall be a country that is eager to learn from others. A country's policy of opening up to the outside world should be carried out after its people's, especially talents' opening up to the outside world. Provided that people are blocked in their own cages of mind, China can never truly open itself up to the world. Consequently, following the policy of opening up to the outside world, we should focus on people and motivate people to be open on new vision, mind, knowledge, and technique. In the face of a rapidly changing international situation, Chinese government has been aggressively promoting open innovation by taking a series of policies in the spirit of reform and innovation. As for higher education, its responsibility lies in cultivating a group of pioneering and international-oriented talents, providing rich reserve forces for our national implementation of innovation driven development strategy and China's important role played in the international arena.

UIR has been committed to cultivating talents with excellent foreign language ability, broad international vision, and solid basic knowledge. Meanwhile, we have been actively promoted a model in both undergraduate and postgraduate education for cultivating pioneering and international-oriented talents. The model features in following four aspects: Firstly, with the "International vision" as the core, majors and curriculums tend to grant students an international strategic thinking; Secondly, in order to improve students' practical abilities and comprehensive quality, we have established cooperative practice bases with enterprises; Thirdly, by offering support for academic and entrepreneurship programs, we aim at training our students' research and problem-solving capabilities; Fourthly, we have long been focusing on the study of international hot-spot issues, scoring a series of major achievements.

The core of talent strategy lies in talent cultivation. That is why we gather here today to explore issues of innovative education and talent cultivation for international organizations. We sincerely hope that all the participants can feel free to air your opinions so as to point a way out for us and make efforts and contribution to global prosperity and human civilization.

Let me conclude by wishing the second Summer Palace Foruma complete success, and I wish all of you a successful Forum and very good health!

Thank you.

CHAPTER

Mr. Joseph W. Bruno

President of Marietta College

玛瑞埃塔学院校长

The Development of Entrepreneurship at Marietta College

What I' d like to do today is to speak to you about the program we are developing at Marietta College on entrepreneurship. Many of us here think about a number of different things, and we often think about starting new businesses and want to emphasize it from the very start. We really think of it as more of a frame on our mind, thinking about new problems, and thinking about solutions, so the problem-solving aspect is a big part of what we are doing. What I would like to do this morning is to talk about 3 different things, one of which is the state of higher education in the United States. And I think we have some challenges, I would like to talk a little about those. And yet, at the top of that, we want to grow even more and have even more success, so the entrepreneurship program is a way to approach some of that.

I want to begin briefly. First, I want to give you a slight introduction of the college.

We are a residential school, a very small college by many standards, as I said earlier; we were founded in 1835, which is in the scope of our nation a long time. We have about 1,200 students. Many of them come from Ohio, but also she consists many from China as well. We compare ourselves to a peer group of 20 different schools, and among that group we have the second highest percentage of international students of the 20 schools. So we are very committed to having students from other parts of the world. Particularly for that, we are able to attract the students from China. That's a great thing for us. We have about 45 academic programs running the range from arts, humanities, social sciences and sciences. We also have 17 intercollegiate athletic teams, which I'll talk a little more about later. Finally, the signature programs in Petroleum Engineering, Leadership, Education, and Physician Assistant Studies. So we may give important contributions to our nation and our region.

But as I said, I think right now in the United States we have some challenges we have to face and pass, and they are really coming from leadership. So right now, we are hearing from some political leaders in our country who view higher education with which I don't entirely agree. One of them is that we should focus predominantly on our students, should focus on choosing a major in college that leads to a job so that that puts a very high premium on science technology. We think that there are many other very important fields, too. There is a course called "cafeteria-style" model where instead of going through a 4-year college education, people in the work force will take a course here, perhaps in welding or accounting. Whenever they need to raise it, they take a course. And we don't think it really contributes to the whole education, the whole person. And the government has talked a little bit about ratings of colleges, which may not be a good idea intrinsically, but we think the grounds they're talking about using are really dubious. But our government, perhaps obviously, has been generous about providing financial aid so that the students can afford college. To this point, financial aid has gone to the students who then have choice of colleges.

There are some talks of signing the financial aid at college first and we disagree with that. And then finally, we all have to stand for accreditation to prove that we were doing what we should be doing and doing it well, and I have no problem with that. But there are some talks recently that the government would be involved in that and none of us think that is not a good idea either. So, to choose one leader in our nation in particular, I have a quote here from our president who talks about education. The part I really stress, the part I tell that one can have a great career without getting a 4-year college education but just get the skill and training. And that I say as the part I disagree with. We do think it's very important that we train students who graduate and can be economically successful and have a great career, but also we think we are doing much more than that as well, so I disagree with what the president said on that, and many of us on higher education do disagree. But I don't want to you leave with your impression that our president is a leader who doesn't appreciate higher education. A few years ago, I had a chance to be present in participating in a ceremony where we awarded degree. President Obama was then Senator Obama. It was just before he got the elect in 2008. As I know, he plays a high value on higher education, and all over our nation leaders do. It's just a matter of what is the best way we achieve higher education. It is there which I disagree a little bit. So I'll talk a little bit about that as I go forward.

If we look at the rating criteria, there are several things that have been discussed and I should say none of these has been put in the entrepreneurship. The first one I can understand that colleges have responsibility to be affordable for our students, and graduation rates I can also understand if a student comes to our college, there should be an expectation that he or she will graduate in a reasonable period of time. The third one that I disagree was very strenuously that we should rate college on how much money their graduates earn after they graduate. Yet we want our students to be successful and to have successful career. But one of the things I mentioned in my first line that the strength of Marietta College is in fact our education program. And it assesses the state affairs in the United States and many other places that although education is as important as we think it is, educators do not make high salary in the United State. So, I think it is a very important service we provide turning out educators and I should tell you that in the State of Ohio of education programs, the Marietta College education program was rated in top 2 in the State. So we have an excellent program that turns out spectacular teachers. They don't make a lot of money but I think they provide tremendous value to our state and to our society. So the salary part I don't particularly care for. Advanced degree is one measure of success. And then finally, many of our students borrow money from the government, and then some of them in other institutions fail to pay it back. So-called default rate, the number of the students who don't pay back their loans, is proposed to be a criterion. So none of these I think is particular burden for the college, I just think they are not the best criteria to evaluate the success of colleges and I'll talk a little bit more about that. But I don't want you to get the impression that because I disagree with those criteria it means that they are problematic for the college. In fact, I want to convince you in the next part. I'll talk that we do very well on many of these fronts.

So, my next line, this data did not come from college, they came from Payscale. com. Completely independent of Marietta College; really has nothing to do with us, but they look very closely across the nation at the salaries the graduates in various colleges make, and then they look how successful the college was in turning out graduates who do in fact get successful careers. If you go through the data which is on over 1,000 institutions and break down by various regions, you can see in our home state, Ohio, there are 42 schools that were evaluated. We have many more than that, but the only look is the 42. Among the 42, Marietta College ranks 3rd in the state in terms of the success our graduates have when they go off into their career. If you broaden your scope a little bit and look at the Midwest region of our nation, in the Midwest, we look at 251 colleges. In their look of 251 colleges, you can see Marietta College was at the top 8%. And when you look nationally at about 1,000 institutions, you can see Marietta College was at the top 11%. So the point I want to stress here is that while I disagree with the idea using salary as the criterion for valuating schools, in no way should that imply you that we are not doing a very good job in that.

None the less, much of what goes into salary depends on what region or country one works in, and what field and other things, and what the family background is. It's a more recent look that comes from Brookings Institution. I present the result on this line. The Brookings, just as you know, is a very highly respected privy research enterprise and not aided with any political party or the government or any other prime enterprise. They praise themselves on doing research which brings out their best opinion regarding what other people might think of those. What they set up to do in the study which was just released about a month ago was to look at the so-called "value added" of college education. In many cases, in other colleges I worked at, we recognize that we brought in talent to wealthy and successful students from well-to-do families. But they were successful when they walked into the door. So in this study, what it's going to try to look at is how much more successful did the college make them than it would have been predicted. So to get that, Brookings looked at the range of demographic information, the region where they grew up, the quality of the high school they attended, family incomes and education, and other things. And they calculated from those background factors, what would have been predicted as the salary for graduates, and then they look at what the salary actually turned out to be, and group those according to colleges. And that difference, looking at the actual over the predicted, is the so-called "value added" that colleges provide above them, beyond what would have been expected for that particular group of students. When you look at the list, it's nationwide over almost 2,500 schools studied here. Some people in this room are representatives. First of all, Mr. Milone is graduated from Colgate University. But you can see that, in the 13th place of 2,488 schools is Marietta College. If you think about the mission of college, which is to educate our students, to bring them from the starting point to a new level of accomplishment or ability or potential, you can see that the college contributes almost a 40% increase of that relative to what would have been predicted. So again, this is a study that is completely independent of the college, but it shows that in terms of this criterion, in our success or preparation for success, we can be very proud of what we were accomplishing. And you can see at the bottom, I've also included some Ivy League schools, with which I'm sure you are familiar as they are great institutions. But as you can see, they don't add as much value according to the study as a small institution like Marietta College. So we make really no apologies by any stricture imagination for disagreeing with the criteria, but we just think they are not particularly germane.

So how is it that our students are so successful, and what markers do we have to show that. One of the career centers is spectacular and you can see all over the work they do every year to try to prepare our students to be successful in the coming year as they search for careers. If we look at that, the graduates of our institution over the past year, and you can see that 87% were successful at career and 12% were in graduate school. So again, our graduates are leaving and finding very great success in their work and life after Marietta College. And then finally, if you come back to the position, the criterion of the loan default, you can see that nationally almost 14% of American students fail to pay back their loans at one point. That's really a problem nationally for us. But if you look at our sector, the private college is only 7%, and if you look at Marietta College, the default rate is under 2%. So again, it's another indication that our students are leaving the college, finding sufficient success, so they can go on and live up their responsibilities, and also forward successful career.

So how is it we do that, and I'll go through these very quickly, but obviously a big part of these are broad-based education, which I think prepares students for anything they're likely to encounter in their life after college. The second is what we call experiential learning. Sectary Wang made a reference this morning to a saying that "Knowledge and practice should go hand in hand", and that's what we call experiential learning. So it is interesting to see that we're thinking about this in the same way, but the focus there is to take what students are learning in classroom and give them out into the rest of the world to practice what they learned. And you'll hear more about that from other speakers from Marietta College later this morning, so I won't talk much about it. We also have a strong belief about Capstone experience. In that project, every student does in his or her senior year before he or she graduates what they've learned over the courses of their last four years, applying for an independent project that they design with the help of faculty member. And it is really a great exercise, allowing our students to demonstrate that they can begin, they can conceive, and design, and executes the project. When they go out into the world, they know how to do that, and they have the evidence for any future imposing they haven't done in the past. I think that is a very important aspect to our success there. And the fourth one which I will spend the rest of my time on is the entrepreneurship program. It is going to be a great contributor to future success.

As I said earlier, we are not simply doing this to start a new business and hope that there will be a perfectly reasonable outcome. One of the things we are seeing in the United States, and I emphasize that it's not just Marietta College; it's across the nation. And to prove that I copy this piece of Harvard Magazine where the person in the picture is a formal colleague, who is the dean of humanities in Harvard. We used to work together in my previous institution. This article, as you can see, the title is *Addressing a Decline in Humanities Enrollment*.

Because of all the emphasis we are putting on science and technology, fewer and fewer students in the United States are willing to pursue other disciplines, particular those in humanities. It's a big part of why I think entrepreneurship program is so important for us and will be in future It allows students to make the connection between the academic disciplines, in particular the humanities and I find it interesting and attractive, and then the bridges convert it to career and success life after college. That's a means and it is an important part of what we are trying to do in entrepreneurship program.

So, those are just a few ideas here about why this is a good idea for Marietta College or put it another way, why the college is well prepared to do this successfully. We do have a strong relationship with our town; we have a great Leadership Program, about which you'll hear more a little bit; we have Executive-in-Residence Program, and you'll hear from both the last two members of those programs. I talked earlier about the Career Center, and I mentioned the Capstones. And also, many leaders on campus are alumni with entrepreneurial experience. So I think it's a very well position to be successful at this.

And here is just the brief outline of what we have planned for this. We are going to have serious academic minors in those that they are developing right now, and we have some internship opportunities, going back to the experiential learning piece. We have other things outside class so-called co-curricular activities; I'll say more about that. And also alternatively, we want to try to found a few small businesses in our town so that graduate can go out, and start business in our town. In order to get this often running, we are hoping to attract outside funding in the last line you can see that. So far, we've been very successful with that and have attracted two grants through the proposal we've read over 300,000 dollars to found the program and get it often running.

The last that I will have in front of you goes to our commitment internship. One of the things for which we are using is the outside funding. We've tried to provide opportunities for our students to get their real world experience, to prepare their knowledge, and the practice as Secretary Wang says. In the great world, some internship we found in college, allowing our students to go out, have their opportunities in the wide world across the nation, and the whole range of fields, including senior students, junior, or even the sophomore. So we're really trying to seek the opportunities and provide the chance for our students to do the outside work.

The other thing that gets them very excited is the co-curricular piece. That is what we call PioPitch, and I have to explain that for a minute. We are called pioneers, because our town was the first town in our region that was founded way back in the 1787. So the people who set up our part of the country which had not been explored by the eastern at that time are known as the pioneers so was the college, we are Marietta College pioneers. I often say that if I know something would be successful for Marietta, it has the word Piopitch in it. The faculty member pictured here is Professor Khorassani in our Economic Department. But you can see from the list, the other people including my two colleagues up here have been very active in trying to get the program off the ground. The whole idea of Piopitch is to bring students, faculties, alumni, local businesses together outside the classroom and have them give talks of the ideas they have, the business they want to start, or in some cases the businesses they had already been running, and the challenges they are facing. This is an important part that goes along with the academic piece that would take place in the classroom. Professor Khorassani was there speaking in an opening section of the first Piopitch, and I should say we have seven Marietta faculty members I believe coming here to teach in the summer. She would be among them, and should be arriving at a later day, not today. She is a great leader of the program, and there you'll see her speaking at the first of those and got them in YouTube videos.

I was going to run some details of that, but it is a long piece. So I think I' ll skip that, and go on next to what our vision is coming out from this program for our students. For some of them, that will in fact be an opportunity to start a new business there on business, so we want to have them learned on how to develop business plans. And we heard something earlier about the emphasis on teaching planning, something we are also doing on the college campus in Marietta. The important part of any enterprise is to have a good plan and places to go forward with, so we help our student to develop those. We will have experts to come in, and we may try to attract Mr. Milone as one of them, but certainly alumni and friends of the college do come back, and they will work with students on business plans and help them improve them, but also pick up those that are most potential, and from the grant money we have attracted, we will help the students get their business started in this city, and provide some other support we have there, and alternately, in the end, to make the program self-perpetuating. We hope and expect that our students who are successful in this way will find a way to pay it back, as we say, or pay it forward to help others in the future to have the same success they have had. So we are just in the process of designing the curriculum of this program, and other parts of it are already in places as I showed you.

But here are some of the things we expect to come out of this and why we are so excited about it. And again, it is not just about starting a business, we want to recruit entrepreneurial students, those are the mindset that says "show me your problem and let me figure out a way to work through it". We do want to make them more successful on whatever career they choose. A local group community is a wonderful group of people, but many people in Marietta are aging, younger people are moving away and older people are moving in, so we want to keep some of our graduates in town to provide young energy in the business community. We want to engage others, and then we keep track of our alumni body, going all the way back to the 1830s, when our first graduates left college, referring to that ongoing group of graduates is the long blue print of Marietta College.

So we are really excited about enhancing the relationship between older alumni and younger alumni, and bringing all that wisdom to bear on the opportunities our young alumni are seeking in their professional lives. But last and certainly, highly important from my perspective is the thing I talked about earlier, which is we really want to be able to demonstrate the students that you can choose a career, you can choose a major in the humanities, or in the social sciences, and still have every expectation and highly successful career.

So again, the idea here is to provide the new minds for our students, to provide a new way of thinking about opportunities in college and how they relate to opportunities after college. What we have seen is that over half of our program graduates within 5 years graduating from college will be working in a job that has nothing to do with the major field they study in college. So the idea is to provide a broad-based experience which allows them to prepare for what we know are going to be some surprises that will come to them in the course of their career. So as you can tell, I am very excited about entrepreneurship as the way for us to prepare students who will be successful and will contribute to the health of the economy and to our nation.

玛瑞埃塔的创业精神

Joseph W. Bruno 玛瑞埃塔学院校长

演讲开头,Joseph Bruno 先生介绍了美国高等教育的现状:如今美国的高等教育正面临着严峻的挑战,整个社会对于就业过于重视,而忽视了大学教育的整体性以及对个人的塑造。面对这些挑战,玛瑞埃塔学院提供的众多校园招聘和实习机会,以及高就业率、读研率和助学贷款的低拖欠率都反映了学院在高等教育领域获得的成功。

Bruno 先生接着分析了成功背后的原因,包括以下四点:第一,广泛的博雅通识教育,体现在非专业领域的课程、对新兴产业的关注以及对口才、写作、分析等综合能力的训练;第二,体验式学习,包括实习、海外留学、独立性研究、服务学习课程等,"知识与实践并肩而行"是学院的不懈追求;第三,每个大四学生都必须完成一个毕业顶点项目,从严格的训练到导师的耐心指导,从综合运用自己四年所学到最后实物成果的产出,无论是对就业还是考研的学生,这都能帮助他们思考自己未来的出路;第四是玛瑞埃塔创业中心,其中包括入学实践工坊、学术性的辅修课程、一系列辅助课程的活动以及创业项目。

随后 Bruno 先生向听众揭示了玛瑞埃塔创业中心成功的要素:首先,玛瑞埃塔有着独特的战略优势,比如与本地企业的紧密联系和众多的实习实践项目;其次是学术方面,学校设置了包括金融、营销、商业发展在内的多项商科核心课程,在实战经验、物尽其用、批判性思维、有效沟通、问题解决、可扩展性方面塑造学生的企业家精神。最后,有经验的校友会针对创业项目的发展进行评估并提供建议。还有种子资金为项目提供启动资金:来自社会和学校两方面的大力支持,对于优秀的项目还会有"提前付款"的奖励条款。

Bruno 先生最后总结道,不应只着眼于本专业领域,开阔的眼界以及丰富的实践机会可以让学生更好地对未来进行准备,促使奇迹发生。玛瑞埃塔为能够培养出在职业上获得成功的学生以及对国家做出巨大贡献的人才感到自豪。

CHAPTER 3

吴 慧

国际关系学院副校长

Wu Hui, Vice President of UIR

人才培养　创新发展　服务社会

人才培养是高等教育的根本任务，是高校一切工作的出发点和落脚点。十八届三中全会明确指出，“要创新高校人才培养机制，促进高校办出特色，争创一流”。国际关系学院如何在新形势下摸索符合自身实际的特色发展道路，为社会培养出合格人才，是一项具有挑战性的艰巨任务。

作为一名在高校工作几十年的老教师，看到中国当前教育界面临的诸多问题后，也深深了解国际关系学院改革发展的难点。对此，我常常陷入沉思。服务社会的合格人才的要素是什么？近年国际关系学院在人才培养方面有哪些可圈可点之处以及有哪些还需改进的措施？我谈点个人看法。

一、培养的学生首先要守诚信、有担当

儒家思想讲人要“修身、齐家、治国、平天下”，修身是基础。只有坚定理想信念、提升道德境界、追求高尚情操，才能成为对社会、对国家、对全人类有用的人。我们的校园不是世外桃源，社会上一些浮躁风气、功利思想会对我们的师生产生影响。所以，我们要培养学生具有踏实的学风，能够孝敬父母，友爱兄弟姐妹和同学，热心社会，关心国家。

我不止一次给我的学生讲一件事：20 多年前我在北京大学求学时，年

逾七旬的导师把我的学长开除了，原因是导师在查找其中期论文的注解时，发现连续三个注释都是错的，从而认定这是一位不值得再去培养的学生。这件事会让我谨记一辈子。现在我们有论文查重制度，有惩治学术不端行为的规范，希望通过耐心教导、制度制约，让我们学生养成诚实守信的良好品德。我认为这比传授专业知识更重要。

另外，由于目前我们的学生大多是独生子女，他们从小就是家庭的中心，有的甚至被溺爱。他们虽然灵活聪明，但勤奋担当不足。所以要注意培养他们对家庭、对社会、对国家的责任感和担当意识。这同样重要。

二、培养方案要立足社会需求、国家需要

衡量一所学校是否办得成功，要看它培养的人才是否符合社会需要。国际关系学院作为一所规模不大、专业相对集中的院校，更是要找准办学定位，集中优势学科培养国家急需人才。

近年我校在原有15个学术学位授权点、一个专业学位授权点的基础上又申请了翻译硕士、法律硕士和警务硕士三个专业硕士学位点。在本科和研究生招生比例上也做了相应调整，使得研究生的培养有一个较大发展。

近期我在微信上看到已毕业学生在给学弟学妹传授经验，其中一句话让我警觉："在大学学的90%以上的理论知识都是用不着的。"我自己没有这个体会，是因为一直在高校做教学科研。且不管这句话的正确程度有多少，至少说明我们在传授知识的过程中对学生的实践能力是有所忽略的。为了使学生能更好适应社会，我们应注重学生知行合一，着力提升其实践能力，坚持专业培养与实践培养相结合。在培养方案的制定方面，除了增加实践课程的学分，还要对外积极拓宽合作渠道，推动学生实践基地建设。2014年以来，我校先后申请建立了北京市市级大学生校外社会实践基地1个，各院系合作办学校外专业实践基地10余个。例如在中国对外翻译出版公司、中国外文局、中国信息安全产品测试认证中心、中国通用技术研究院等单位设立了教学实践基地，以保证专业硕士培养质量得到全面保证。我们还注重把校内实践教学、校外实习实践和学生自主创新结合起来，希望能够构

建全方位的实践育人模式,为创新人才培养搭建广阔的平台。

三、人才培养体系的特点是坚持“一制三化”

我校在2012年就明确提出要把“导师制、小班化、个性化和国际化”为基本框架开展我校教育教学改革的思路。不仅实行研究生导师制,还实行了本科生导师制。对于专业学位硕士研究生实行双导师制。目前我校外语本科教学班均能保持在每班20人左右,各专业教学班不超过30人。

我也注意到本次夏宫论坛主题的副标题是:国际组织人才培养与发展。作为“国际”打头的高校,理应培育具有国际竞争力的学生。一次参加某个会议,有学者在感叹:我国在重要国际组织任职的人数只有区区几百人,而荷兰却有逾万人。所以,为了顺应经济全球化以及中国“走出去”战略,我们需要培养具有国际竞争力,能够服务国际社会的人才。

近年来,我校继续加强引进海外学成归国教师,鼓励教师开展国际交流和参与国际学术活动。特别是加大资金支持力度,鼓励教师独立或合作开发国际化课程,引进国外原版教材,扩大双语课程授课范围等。同时,与美国、法国、以色列、日本等国多所院校签订合作协议,增加外派交换生数量。例如,我校与丹麦奥尔堡大学开展的“中国与国际关系”联合硕士项目受到中丹两国教育部门的认可和支持,中丹双方的毕业硕士研究生已突破40人。

四、培养目标应是身心健康、积极向上、学有所长的人才

以德行为基础,以理论和实践相结合的专业课程提升能力,再辅以“大学生学术支持计划”以及多项学科和文体竞赛,让学生真正得以个性化成才。

我校自2012年建立“国际关系学院大学生支持计划”以来,先后投入科研经费近400万元,学生科研立项超过900项;其中,以2014年“研究生学术支持计划”立项为例,研究生立项达96项,参与学生超过350人次,立项金额近45万元,基本达到每名研究生均独立主持或参与一项学生科研

课题。

2014年，学校还结合研究生教育改革，出台了《国际关系学院研究生“三助”工作管理办法》及其《实施细则》，通过设立学生助教、助研和助管岗位，提供配套资源和资金，从体制上将研究生的教学和科研双重培养模式结合起来。2015年先后有69名研究生从事“三助”岗位，管理实施和培养效果显著。

近年由我校主办的全国大学生政府采购论坛、国际关系学院研究生“国关·润远”学术论坛和“润贤”系列学术沙龙、大国关系研究方法讲习班、模拟联合国、APEC论坛和博鳌亚洲论坛等一大批学术和科研实践类活动成为校内外学生交流、沟通和锤炼学术能力的平台，涌现出不少优秀学术和实践成果。例如法律系同学组队参加今年的“国际刑事法院模拟法庭比赛”，取得全国前三的成绩并代表中国去荷兰海牙参加了全球比赛。

近年来，国际关系学院在创新人才培养方面进行了一系列有益探索，有成绩，但更有差距。未来要做的、可做的事情还很多，任重道远，让我们一起努力！谢谢大家！

Serving Society through Talent Cultivation and Innovative Development

Talent development is the basic task of higher education, which is also the starting point and purpose of all work in universities. The Decision on Major Issues Concerning Comprehensively Deepening Reforms adopted at the Third Plenary Session of the 18th CPC Central Committee clearly pointed out that we shouldinnovate mechanism of talents development in colleges and universities, striving to be the world's top higher institutions. Thus under new circumstances, it is a challenging task for the University of International Relations to develop a distinctive development path and to cultivate qualified talents for the society.

As an experienced teacher in university, having seen numerous challenges China is facing now, I fully understand the difficulties of UIR'S reform and development. Thus I always contemplate: What are the necessary qualities that a person should have to serve the society? In recent years, what are the achievements that UIR has accomplished and what are the improvements UIR needs to make? I would like to offer my personal opinions.

First of all, we need to cultivate honest and responsible students.

Confucianism advocates to" cultivate your moral character, regulate your family, commit yourself to the country's development and make all peaceful!", which indicates that cultivating moral characters is the basis. Only by conforming to one's ideal and faith and elevating one's moral level can one be truly useful to society, to the country and to the mankind. Our campus is not a land of idyllic beauty. Snobbishness and materialism will sometimes pose negative effect on both our teachers and students. Therefore, we should teach students to be steady and sure in study, to love their parents, to love their brothers and sisters, and to care for our society and country.

There is one incident that I have been telling my students more than once. It happened about twenty years ago when I studied in Beijing University. My advisor, a man over seventy years old, expelled one of the senior students, because he found three annotation mistakes in the student's midterm paper, thus regarding the student as not worth cultivating. I will remember this for the rest of my life. Nowadays we have paper re-check system and rules to punish academic dishonesty. This aims to develop honesty and good moral characters among students, which I believe is even more significant than professional knowledge.

Moreover, currently most of our students are the only child in their family, who grows up as the focus of the family and is even spoiled. Clever as they are, they lack assiduity and a sense of responsibility. Therefore, it is also important to cultivate their sense of responsibility for family, society and our nation.

The cultivation plan should be based on social and national needs.

Whether a university is successful depends on whether the talents it cultivates can meet the need of the society. As a relatively small university with focused majors, UIR has to identify the orientation of the university and concentrate on the advantageous disciplines to cultivate the talents urgently needed.

In recent years, in addition to the 15 academic programs, our university has applied 3 Master's degree programs on Interpreting and Translation, Law and Policing. The proportion of the number ofundergraduates and graduates students admitted has been adjusted accordingly, which has improved graduate education remarkably.

Recently I saw some posts onWechat, which are about experiences shared by graduated students to their younger fellow. One of their remarks caught my attention, it says, more than 90% of the theoretical knowledge we learned in university is useless. I don't feel it myself though because I have always been doing scientific research in university. However, no matter how credible this remark is, it at least demonstrates our negligence on students' practical ability. In order to help our students adjust better to the society, we need to practice the Chinese old saying "knowledge and action should go hand in hand". Besides, we need to focus on improving students' practical ability and combine professional development with practical development. When making cultivation plans, besides increasing the credits for practical courses, we should spare no efforts to broaden external cooperation channels and promote the construction of students' practical bases. Since 2014, our university has established one Beijing undergraduates' extracurricular base and more than ten department practical bases. In order to fully guarantee the quality of graduate education, we have set up practical education bases in China Translation and Publishing Corporation, China International Publishing Group, China Information Security Products' Test Certification Center, China General Technology Institute and so on. We also concentrate on combining campus practical education, extracurricular internship and students' independent innovation, hoping to establish a comprehensive cultivation model and create a broad platform for nurturing new talents.

The feature of the cultivation system of talents is "one-system and three aims"

Our university made it clear in 2012 that we shall carry on the education reform within aframework based on tutorial system, small-sized class education, individualization, and internationalization. We carry out the tutorial system for both-graduates and undergraduates, as well as double-tutors system for the master of professional degree. At present, every class of undergraduates majoring in foreign languages in our university only has about 20 students, and the classes of other majors are about 30 at most.

I have also noticed that the subtitle of the theme of this forum is "Talent-Cultivation and Development for International Organizations". As a university whose name begins with "International", we need to cultivate internationally competitive students. I once attended a meeting, hearing one scholar complaining that China only has a few hundreds of people who work in important international organizations, while Netherland has over ten thousand. Therefore, in order to adjust to globalization and China's strategy of "going out", we need to cultivate talents who have international competitiveness and the ability to serve international community.

In recent years, our university continues to introduce more excellent teachers who have overseas backgrounds and encourage faculties to launch and get involved into international academic exchange activities. Particularly, we also attach great importance to offering more financial support, motivating teachers to develop global courses independently or collaboratively, bringing in original learning materials from abroad, enlarging the scope of bilingual education and so on. Meanwhile, UIR has signed the cooperation agreements with many universities in foreign countries, including United States, France, Israel and Japan, and the number of exchange students keeps growing accordingly. For instance, the joint Master's program, "China and International Relations" between our university and Aalborg University in Denmark has received recognition and support from education departments in two countries. So far, more than 40 students from China and Denmark in this program have received Master's degree.

Our goal is to cultivate talents that are healthy, positive and professional.

Here we have major courses that combine theory and practice, Research and Training Programand various subject and sports competition. These activities truly lead to students' individual success.

Since the Research and Training Program for University of International Relations was established in 2012, we have invested in nearly 4 million research funds and launched more than 900 research projects. Among them, take the 2014 Research and Training Program for graduate students for example, there are more than 350 students participating in 96 research projects, the funds of which have reached 45 thousands Yuan. This means that nearly every graduate student independently organizes or takes part in one research project.

In 2014, along with the education reform of graduate school, we have issued the Management Rules of Graduate Students' Three Types of Jobs, which are teaching, research and administrative assistant. By providing these jobs, relevant resources and funds, we aim to cultivate both the ability of teaching and conducting research in graduate students. In 2015, 69 graduate students have participated in this program, which turns out to be very effective.

In recent years, a number of academic and research projects hosted by UIR have provided a platform for students to communicate, exchange ideas and improve their academic ability. These activities include Government Procurement Forum for National University Students, UIR RUNYUAN Academic Forum and Runxian academic salon, International Relations Research Method Seminar,

Model United Nations, Model APEC Forum and Model Boao Forum. In these activities, numerous academic and research achievements have been reached. For example, a team from the law department broke into top three in the National ICC Moot Court competition and represented China to participate in the international competition, which was held in Hague, Netherlands.

In recent years, UIR has carried out a series of explorations to cultivate innovative talents. We have accomplished some achievements but this is a heavy responsibility and we still have a long wayto go. We will continue fighting for this cause and I hope all of us can work together!

Thank you!

CHAPTER 4

Mr. Mark A. Miller

Dean of Marietta College
玛瑞埃塔学院教务长

Innovation Education: A Multi-faceted Approach to Preparing Leaders for Global Engagement in theTwenty-First Century

Our cheer today is "go blue, go white". Why go blue, go white? Our school color is your school color. But it is more than that, it is talking about how our countries can work together, our schools work together. And I always think about the way that our schools work together as a micro pattern of our countries work together.

When I grew up in the United States, there would be no chance that a university from the United States and a university from China would be having the collaboration that we have today. You've always known that the United States and China has some type of good relationship, and that is an important thing to remember because when we look at the globe today, we see terrible things happening in Indonesia, in the United States, happening around the world, all because people cannot get along. But I think China and US have shown the world that countries can get along. And that is what we are talking about today and tomorrow: how can China prepare itself to move on in the global platform.

What I' m going to talk today is markets and methodology as relate to higher education. I think there are different ways of thinking what markets are when we are in college. There are three kinds of markets that the US students have to engage in. There is the marketplace of ideas, and that is a very important marketplace. Nobody pays you to think. As we heard earlier today, one of your students said that 90 percent of what I learned doesn' t seem like to be useful. When I taught mathematics, I told my students, about 100 percent of what you are going to learn in this class, you will never use it again, but it doesn' t mean it is not useful. When you are taking the classes, we are preparing you to think. No pays for you, but if you don' t participate in it, you are not going to be paid in the next marketplace, that is the marketplace of commerce. That is what we think marketplace would be, we think it is all about trade, selling and buying. That is an important thing but it is just one of the three marketplaces. And then it is the marketplace of social responsibility and a marketplace about exchange. So how do we exchange ideas, how do we exchange goods and services, how do we exchange social responsibilities for a better society? In American colleges, we have different ways to approach this: the first you think is academic engagement, and that is a fancy way of saying the traditional classroom, but that is only one part of learning; there is residential learning, which is learning when you actually living in a school; there is co-curricular involvement, the things that you learn outside the classroom; and there is of course experiential education, the education outside but still organized. So I' m going to talk about these three marketplaces and these four accesses.

Ⅰ. The marketplace of ideas

The whole market of the marketplace of ideas is free exchange. A free exchange means that I can provide whatever I want to provide, and you are going to tell me how valuable you think that thing is. If it is not valuable, you don't have to buy it; but if it is valuable, you have to give me something of equal value in exchange for it. And without the marketplace of ideas, the other two so-called marketplaces are not true because we have to base these on an intellectual framework. I want to mention a few things that I think are important for the marketplace of ideas.

One of the reasons that the marketplace of ideas is so important is that good ideas in the marketplace drive out bad ideas. In other words, you have an idea and I have an idea, if your idea is better than mine, your idea will eventually rise in value and mine go down in value. In the marketplace, good ideas turn to go to the surface and bad ideas turn to go down. Look at the globe, look at how my country has changed, look at how your country has changed, and look at how the society around us has changed. It turns out that good ideas drive out bad ideas. When I say "good" and "bad", I don't say "good" in terms of "morally good" and bad in terms of "morally bad". I say "good" as what the society values.

Another thing important is the next point, the majority is often wrong. Here these two things are in tension with each other. Because good ideas drive out bad ideas, those good ideas are shared by the majority of people. The majority ideas are eventually going to change the minority, but often the majority is wrong. So what I am to emphasize in the marketplace of ideas is that even if I win, I need to listen to people who lose. So we have to have the majority rule but the minority rights. And many problems have no perfect solution, so we have to look for a best-fit.

There are three things we do to prepare our students to thrive. We try to provide academic rigor, we try to make sure our students to think clearly. Academic rigor is important because when you enter the marketplace of commerce, you have to be rigorous, otherwise you can't survive. We also try to promote the free and open exchange of viewpoints within our campus, within our classroom. We try to make our students think that they don't have to agree with their professors. And then we try to promote critical thinking. It is basically holding two conflicting ideas and trying to find the values of both ideas.

About marketplace of ideas, I want to talk about academic engagement. Arithmetic, geometry, music, astronomy, rhetoric, grammar and logic were the seven things that were input in an educated person when the idea of universities were first found in Europe. Marietta College values that column of seven traditional liberal arts and sees it a way of preparing students for moving beyond life at the college. We identify another seven ways which we call "institutional learning outcomes": artistic literacy, communication, critical thinking, diversity, ethical citizenship, inquiry, quantitative reasoning. We hope our students to be highly professional in these seven ways of thinking when they graduate. So we try to construct our curriculum around these seven ideas.

I want to mention about the experiential education. There are four types of experiential education in America: study abroad, investigative studies, internships and service learning. Study abroad is not taking a vacation but learn about how other people in another country learn about this concept. And the second thing we talk about is the investigative studies. When we say investigative studies in Marietta College, our students apply for, and if they are successful, they win a grant to work with the professor on a research project or a creative project over the summer. The students are paid more than the faculties, and that is because the students do more of the work than the faculties do.

Ⅱ. The marketplace of commerce

The second marketplace is of course the marketplace of commerce. Good ideas may drive out bad ideas, but oddly, bad products can drive out good products. And here is an example of bad products driving out good products: When the tape players were first developed in the 80s, there were basically two models, one is a model developed by Sony Corporation called Betamax, and the other is the VHS, the video home system. And anybody who knows anything about television and film said the Sony product was the better product, but the VHS product was cheaper. And eventually Sony, who had the better product, didn't get a part in the market. That's one example of a bad product driving out a good product. So we have to prepare students to think that way, in other words, it is not enough to say that my product is the best product, you have to be able to convince people that your product is worth buying. And often, good things cost more than bad things, so if you have a product, you are going to tell a story that why your product is worth extra money than the bad product.

And the second is that we have the same saying in America that "the customer is always right". That means when you are providing a service, if your customers complain, don't complain back to them; if your customers think you have a problem, don't make excuses, solve the problem. But the reality is, the idea that "the customer is always right" is often wrong. The customers are often wrong, but they want to be treated like that they are always right. So we have to prepare our students how to interact with their customers, co-workers when they enter the marketplace of commerce. When you know they are wrong, you are right, it is not enough to be right, it is also important to make your customers, you co-workers to work together with you.

Again, many problems have no perfect solutions; you have to move for a best-fit. That is exactly the same with the marketplace of ideas. Just like the marketplace of ideas, we have to find a best-fit to make our companies working together, our people working together, even it is not perfect.

And how do we prepare our students to this way of thinking, we have three ideas. One is we try to promote creative problem solving. Our mathematical books have no examples, only questions. And we spend the whole semester looking up the questions and try to answer the questions together in a very creative way to discover well-known mathematical ideas. The old way of thinking is that you read what the old people told you and you tell your children the same story. But if all I do is to tell you what my father told me, what if my father was wrong? We have to think creatively to solve the problems. And then we've got the oral and written communication skills. We make every student in the first year attend classes of oral communication and written communication, even those students are not native English speakers. We think it is important to prepare people to communicate in order to thrive in the marketplace. And again we think it is important to have students involved in individual and collaborative projects. Students have to work individually and collaboratively in the same time.

We would engage students academically for the marketplace of commerce. Marietta College was originally charted to provide institution in "the various branches of useful knowledge." No matter what students learn in Marietta College, it has to be useful. And the major thing we do for experiential education for commerce is internship.

Ⅲ. The marketplace of social responsibility

The third marketplace is the marketplace of social responsibility. A marketplace is where things are exchanged freely and openly. We can exchange our ideas freely and openly, and if we can do that, we can exchange goods and services freely and openly. But in some point we have to realize as a global society, that there are things beyond ideas and materials. Social responsibility needs to be exchanged between and among people, colleges, universities and nations.

Commerce and social responsibility do not have to go against each other; they can go together very well. Some of our largest corporations in the United States are the leaders of social responsibilities. When I say social responsibility I mean that making sure the world we live is good for all of us. Good citizen responsibility is good for business.

In the US, we often have a disconnection between our non-profit sector and our career-driven sector. When we talk about non-profit, we talk about institutions whose existence is not to generate more money, whose existence is to generate education, house, poverty relief or anything that will help the less fortunate. And what we are trying to get students to understand is that one can have a very meaningful career working in the non-profit sector.

Many problems have solutions that rely on for-profits and non-profits together. And the three ways we want students to thrive in the marketplace is social responsibility including civic engagement, intra-community living and extra-community living. A project we started just a couple of years ago is a project called Project NextGen, short for next generation. This is a project of your generation, your age. It is about young people living involved in non-profit leadership. In this program we train students to be not the volunteers but the leaders in local non-profits in the Marietta area so that when they graduate they can serve as leaders in the non-profit industry. And if you look at the things we have in the NextGen Project that we teach students for non-profit leadership, you will find they are very similar to what you need to learn in for-profit leadership: finances and fund-raising, information technology, human resources, marketing, networking and advocacy, operations and governance, programs and planning.

创新教育:21世纪培养全球事务领导者的多方面途径

Mark Miller 玛瑞埃塔学院教务长

Mark Miller 先生的演讲围绕与高等教育有关的市场与方法论展开。据 Miller 先生介绍，美国学生们会接触参与的市场有三种:第一种是思想市场,第二种是商品市场,而第三种是社会责任市场。为使学生们做好进入这三种市场的准备,玛瑞埃塔提供了四种不同的途径:学术教育、住宿教育、合作课程和经验教育。

Miller 先生首先着重介绍了思想市场。他表示,在思想市场,思想是无价的,并且是可以免费交换的。好的思想终将留下,而坏的思想则会慢慢消失。所谓“好”与“坏”并不意味着道德意义上的崇高与低下,因为多数人往往是错的。因此需要明确一个观点,即少数服从多数,但少数仍有发言权。多数情况下,很多问题都没有完美的解决方案,但人们要寻找最适合的方案。关于如何让学生做好准备进入思想市场,学院采取了三种方法:一是保持学术上的严谨;二是自由公开的思想交流;三是培养批判性思维。

接下来 Miller 先生介绍了商品市场的情况:在商品市场,好的商品会消失,而留下的是坏的商品,这一点与思想市场恰恰相反。这是因为好的商品比坏的商品更贵。而“顾客永远是对的”这一观点却是错的:事实上,顾客经常是错的,只是他们希望自己永远是对的。同思想市场一样,大多问题没有完美的解决方案,人们也要去寻找最适合的方案。对于让学生更好地适应商品市场,学院同样采用三种方法:一是创造性地解决问题;二是训练沟通技巧;三是鼓励学生做个人项目和合作项目。

最后,Miller 先生提到了社会责任市场:商品和社会责任并不冲突,因此学院鼓励学生们在非盈利机构工作、做领导者。很多问题也要靠盈利机构和非盈利机构合作解决。为了让学生们在社会责任市场更好地进入角色,学院提供了市民参与、校内团体、校外团体三种方案。

CHAPTER 5

M r. Andy Zelleke

Harvard Business School
哈佛大学商学院 MBA 首席教授

Empathy, Innovation and Value Creation

Good morning, everybody ! I' m delighted to be here. I' m really thrilled to be here, it' s my second time—I was here two years ago, and Professor Liu was kind enough to invite me a second time, so thank you so much Prof. Liu, and thank you for your hospitality. I want to also thank all of you, because I noticed it' s Sunday morning, I know that there are many other things you could be doing, and so I' m very appreciative that you are here.

Xiaoxiong has already basically given you everything I wanted to say, so I can just stop here. Now I will actually continue for a little bit. I will try to be concise and respect your schedule.

Let me start by taking a poll. In Harvard Business School (HBS) by the way, we very rarely lecture—we engage with the students. So I' mgonna do a bit of that today. So I' m going to start by taking a poll about three things:

First Iwanna give a sense of what your primary interests are, professionally, what you expect to be doing as your profession. How many of you, raise your hand to answer this, expect to do business in some fashion? OK, just a few of you, not too many. So not too many entrepreneurs? OK, what about government service? How many people plan to go into government? Just a couple of you? Teaching? How many people don't know yet what they want to do? A few more of you. What about the rest of you? Just pull it out, what you want to do? Gentleman in the green shirt, what do you want to do professionally, do you know? (Audience: Maybe a lawyer? Or others, I'm not sure.) Maybe law school? Lawyer? OK, thank you! That's one poll. I got to say that it didn't work out very well (laugh), let me try a different one.

Imagine that Prof. Liu has arranged for you two world-class speakers, talking about two different topics. One topic is that the speaker is going to teach you to become a world-class speaker. The other seminar is that the speaker is going toteach you to become a world-class listener. And the problem is that the two seminars, because of the speakers' schedules, are at the same time. So you can't take both, you have to make a choice which to attend. I need everybody to take five seconds to think about it, which one of the two you are going to attend. I'm going to ask you to signify by standing up. So first, I would like everybody who would choose to attend the seminar on becoming a world-class listener to stand up now. What about those who choose the other? It's about fifty-fifty, but I think you might be influenced by the people in the front row (Most of the teachers in the front row stood to choose the former one). The truth is, when I was your age, if someone asks me this question, I would say to myself, you gotta be kidding—of course the world-class speaker. Why? Because I would say to myself, even though I am reasonably OK with speaking, there's always room for improvement, and that's something really important. But listening? I know I don't listen that much, but I can anytime I want to. Anytime that's important, I'll just listen better. You guys are a lot more mature than I was at your age. Listening is very important, and that ties with my topic of the role of "empathy" in innovation and value-creation. And I will explain that some more.

Let me just say what I'm going to do very briefly. I'm going to start by making a few comments about leadership. I will give a very quick overview about the course I teach, that is the "Leadership and Innovation" in HBS. And I want to then talk about the major role that I believe empathy plays in three specific contexts. The first context is, in the business world, innovation in products and services, which ties withthe course I teach in HBS. The second context, more generally, is in business negotiations. And the third topic is in international relations and foreign policies. We are now in the University of International Relations, I will also say something about this topic.

A few comments about leadership:

First, when I was a freshman in Harvard College, before going there, I was the class president in my high school. It's a very prominent high school in New York City. When I went to Harvard College, there was an opportunity in the first year of college—to run for the president of the freshmen class in Harvard College. I thought that would be a good thing to do. So I ran for president, there were three candidates, and I finished second. I was heartbroken about this. And I started to ask myself why I was heartbroken about this? And the true answer is I thought it would have been cool to be the president of a freshmen class of Harvard College. And it took me a while to figure out that's actually not a true reason for occupying a senior leadership role. You have to want to do something more thanthat. I did want to do something to improve the students' experience and etc. But honestly, that was secondary. My primary reason for wanting to be in a senior leadership role was ego, which is the dumbest reason of all to want to be in a leadership role. When President Bruno decided to accept the appointment as the President of Marietta College, he didn't do that because he wanted to be a president, he did that because he knew that was the position through which he could become extremely impactful in improving the life of the students and others at Marietta College, and he has done a great job for doing that. That's the right reason to want to be a senior leader.

So I made the first observation about leadership that the purpose of leadership is to be in service for somebody else, not to gratify your own ego. The purpose of leadership is to associate yourself with a cause that you believe in, and to have impact in relation to that cause. So you are a servant as a leader, as opposed to be a master as a leader. Very important, I came a little bit late to come to that realization, I should have realized it as a freshman at college, but I was not yet mature enough to do that.

Acouple of other observations about leadership, many of them come from important scholars at Harvard University, but not exclusively there. First, leadership does not require that you occupy a senior leadership authority role. Leadership is better understood as being acts of leadership that can be perpetrated by anybody at any level in an organization, in a society, or in a community. So everybody should view themselves potentially a leader, regardless of a formal authority position they may or may not hold.

One important thing that leaders do is that they shape a culture in organizations, in societies, in families, at any level. The single most important thing leaders do is they create and shape a culture that in turn shapes the behavior of many people thereafter, also in a constructive and functional way. (It's a) very important aspect of leadership. And again, anybody at any level in an organization or a team can do their part to shape a culture.

Next thing I want to say about leadership is that cognitive intelligence, measured by what we call "IQ", is not the most important determinant of leadership capacity. It's obviously helpful to have cognitive intelligence above certain threshold. But you don't have to be Dr. Einstein, in terms of brilliance to be a very effective leader. What we have counter-understand come to understand is that emotional intelligence, what we call "EQ", becomes much more important after a certain threshold level of cognitive intelligence "IQ". And EQ consists of a number of things; I won't go into all of it. But, certainly, self-awareness—

understandingyourself, understanding your strengths and weaknesses, passion and etc. is a big part of it. Empathy is (also) a big part of it. Xiaoxiong already gave a good sense of what I mean by empathy. But at the heart of it, it is to equally understand the perspectives of any emotions of others. Leaders are focused on achieving results that may qualify better for the people with whom they are identifying.

I want to say a couple of things about leadership that connected up with innovation and value-creation. It's been taken for granted now the distinction between management on the one hand, and leadership on the other. And the way that is typically expressed is that management is more about coping with complexity, and leadership is more about coping with change. And in fast-changing environments, like the one we are in today, where technology is progressing at an extraordinary pace, the need for leadership as opposed to management is quite obvious.

And the second connection between leadership and innovation I want to make—this is also one of my favorite academic definitions of all times—this has to do with my colleague Howard Stevenson's definition of entrepreneurship. Professor Stevensondoesn't define entrepreneurship as start-ups and something like that. What he defines entrepreneurship to be is the pursuit of opportunity, without regard to the resources they currently control. Another way to put that is, entrepreneurship is the pursuit of opportunity, unlimited or unconstrained by the resources currently controlled. I would say that is a very good definition of entrepreneurial leadership, which is the most important type of leadership. Because it is a kind of leadership that is most focused on dealing with change. And what that definition highlights is—unlike a trustee who focuses on the assets under his or her control inside an organization, and obsesses about not losing value and preserving the principal, and not like a manager who focuses and obsesses on "how can I deploy the resources under my control to create value"—the entrepreneur or the entrepreneurial leader obsesses not about what resources are inside or outside the organization, but rather, obsesses about what are the opportunities out there or extraordinary value creation. What are those opportunities? Where goes the opportunity? If I can identify them, I1l have the ladder about the simply necessary resources, the human capital, the financial capital, as sediment in order to pursue that opportunity. My point about the identity in opportunity for maximum: value creation.

Okay, when we start there, I will share a couple of things of the course that I teach. The mission of Harvard Business School is not creating successful business people, the people that make a lot of money. All over the world might make abusiness school of that. The mission of Harvard Business School is educating leaders to make a difference in the world. So this course is very much about bringing to life about Harvard Business School's mission, because Harvard Business School was founded in 1908, so it' s more than a hundred years, which in America is a long time. For almost the past a hundred years, it has simply used a certain method of teaching

—the case method, which is that the student reads a 10 to 15 pages of case with a whole bunch of financial exhibits. And then there is a lot of discussion in the room, and the debate is over what is the correct cause of action, what is the optimal cause of action for the central decision maker. That's the case method, the Harvard Business School version.

And at a certain point, the leadership of the school decided, if our mission is in fact educating leaders to make a difference in the world. It is great that everybody is so well prepared at two years of Harvard Business School education to talk about what they would do imagining themselves to be in the shoes of the case protagonist. That's certainly a great wealth of the school that its graduates are very highly regarded, etc. Well the dean, still be in my judgment, concluded that if the purpose/ mission of the school was educating leaders to make a difference in the world, what the school needs to do better was to give actual leadership experience to students and that's what this big institutional curriculum reform is about creating a few courses, four years ago, I've been teaching this course for the past four years and now the leadership of this courses.

Fewisn't acquitive stands for few emersion experiences in leadership in developing. And the basic idea is to learn about leadership not by talking about what you would do but by actually doing, and working in teams, because most of the hard work in the real world or every kind of organization is done not in a solo activity but rather in teams. And it would seem so self-manage, with a faculty that do not put a lot of guidance on organizing your leadership in this way or that way that we tell students listening tests will get it done, figure out what I can do. And we coach them for the issue that come from them, and we give them real problem still this amount of simulations you should not exercise this real challenges in the real world that they focus on. Three parts of the field, and I'm probably a leader of FIELD 2, which are lot of are as FIELD 1 let's call it foundational, and I won't say much about that part.

In FIELD 2, we basically set all 940 Harvard Business School students in January of each year around the world to various emerging market destinations where they work on actual projects with actual companies, with the most part they are working on developing products or services for those companies. That's a task to whichthey have to bring a lot of creative ideas. Our students are very talented. They have very good experience after their undergraduate years. They are very confident, very capable. They are very good at applying analytic technique to make optimal decisions. What they are not necessarily very experienced or confident about is generating new ideas, innovative ideas. That's what you need when you are creating new products. That is what this course is about: giving them some values, giving them the tools to develop confidence in their own creativity and ability to innovate, to create value. That is FIELD 2.

In FIELD 3, we put them in different teams, and we tell them: "You have 14 weeks to run a start-up business." This is not a business plan competition; you actually have to develop ideas, and then with your idea, go out into the market place and actually sell your products or services. At the end, there is a panel of extraordinary judges who will evaluate your business.

We try to get the students to be more creative, and to have more confidence in their capacity to add value by being creative. The methodology to teach them is "human-centered design". I will give you an example. One of the projects that students worked on, a six-person team of students went to India. The appliance of the idea was developing a new service or customary experience with Harvey Davidson of India.

Harvey Davidson is a well-known American motorcycle manufacturer with a very strong brand. It represents American whole lifestyle of the U. S. They sell their products around the world. In India, they try to let women become more interested in buying Harvey Davidson motorcycles and being part of the Harvey Davidson cultural experience. Thestudents team had never been to India before, started out knowing nothing about India, nothing about motorcycles. Their job was essentially to develop a new concept. The company whose business every single day was trying to figure out what motorcycles are. These students' job was to come up with new and creative ideas to sell motorcycles. They did a very good job. I can't talk about the statistics because it is confidential. But I will give you an example.

How did the students do that? That is where "human-centered design" comes in. We gave them some tools. The heart of these tools was to design a thinking method. First, you can't just let six smart Harvard Business School students sitting in a room applying analytical techniques to generate new, innovative ideas, like a company who does his business every day. You can't do that. Analysis will not get you there. The first step in "human-centered design" is to go out and learn in a very deep way about the customers. These students went out and spent time with Indian women and the target customer segment to understand what was missing from their motorcycle buying experience, to understand how they could add value tothese women's lives and how the very good experience of Indian men who bought these motorcycles could be translated onto women. So the first step is to spend time with customers, observing them, deeply understanding them, developing empathy with them, almost like standing in their shoes and seeing the world these people see.

Second step, once they have that deep understanding of the customers, we gave them some tools to aggregate their materials, to help them generate very good, creative new ideas. The first thing you are going to do is to generate a lot of ideas, before you use analysis to choose the best. Being able to generate a lot of ideas requires some process and some cultural features that make it likely that people who won't be ridiculous to their peers or none of us is comfortable throwing out ridiculous selling ideas. The point is to get a lot of ideas, including some wild ones even if none of wild one proves ultimately to be viable or feasible. Some of the wild ideas are often containing eternal of insights that you can take model to make it more realistic and programmatic. The next step of this process is to go back out to the customers again, and find some ways, like a video or a prototype, to show thecustomers your idea. You get an additional feedback from customers; these feedback may be included in your ideas. After all these processes: understanding the customer, brainstorming, wild creative ideas, translating your ideas to customers, finally at the end of this process, you come up with your best idea that has enough feedback from customers. With this method, it is not possible for students to conclude with certainty that it is the best idea, but they are able to give a pretty good, promising idea to the company, and it is for the company to test the idea in the market.

We take them to China; we have fifty students in Beijing, that was not the past January but two Januaries ago. We have two cities in China this year, Shanghai and Chengdu. We havealso India, Brazil, South Africa, Indonesia, the Philippines, Turkey, Argentina, Peru, Cambodia and Morocco. That's where we take all these students. It's a huge majestic undertaking for our students to set off in the four years. They have well behaved in such an international incidence. The purpose of the project is we are trying to take these very smart, very capable, very analytic student and we are trying to unleash their creativity. Because what we need tomorrow is more creativity, more innovation, and not just good analysis. That's what the focus of this course is.

Now we have talked about the FIELD course. At the end of the day, we need our decision makers—whatever decision—making process we are talking about, in the political realm, in the business realm, decision making in company, decision making in sports team, whatever the context—we want the best decision to bemade. If we just focus on the process of making decision, we miss the part at the center of creativity and innovation.

We need to make sure that on the menu of possible choices that can be chosen from by the decision makers, we want the ideas to be there, to be possible. It's very essential that you, as the talented young people, that it doesn't matter what kind of organization you are in, it doesn't matter how your hierarchy is, it doesn't matter how much appropriate authority there is in your organization. What the superior leaders want from you is what's real in your mind; they don't want you to say something just to please them. The American political system is not typically hierarchical. The president has much power obviously, but the president can't do whatever he wants to do, because the Congress may want something else, the Supreme Court may want something else, and the states in the US remain much power. So it is very difficult for the president in the US to get something done. But, even in the Business School, we are imitating a system quite hierarchical. The CEO, chief executive officer, in the 500 top companies in the

US, is the boss. It's not a cabinet government, it's not a collective government, the CEO is the boss that makes decisions. But the CEO, at the process prior to the decision is made, wants all the good ideas, whether they are supported by the CEO initially or not. Might you be a very senior member of an organization, am I correct on that? The CEO likes to ask "what is your opinion?" These ideas are subject to the CEO to decide. It's everybody's responsibility to create ideas and put them on the table, as may be potentially promising, good. That is appropriate at every level of the organization.

OK, let me just say a couple of things about the context. First, in negotiation, this is the notion you need, be able to put yourself in the shoes of somebody else. The best negotiators are not those most articulated, persuasive, it's the people who have listened very carefully to the people sitting on the other side of the table and fully understand their interests and their priorities, because that understanding, just like that of the customers in the context, that understanding becomes the material that can be used to creatively put together the comprehensive transaction into a deal that actively satisfy the interest of the other party as well as that of yourself. In order to do it, not only pay attention to the other party, you shall also be clear on your own interest, what you want, since you need their consent to get deal done. So value creation and innovation comes from deals that requires listening carefully to the interests and needs of the other party and only then can you use that material to draft the terms of the deal that makes both sides happy. That's true for every kind of business negotiation.

And the last context to mention is the negotiation in foreign policy. The problemin international politics is that there is so few new ideas, so few creative ideas. It is particularly difficult for anybody to articulate any new idea.

There's a senior colleague at Harvard Business School called Michael Porter, he's perhaps the most famous person at Harvard Business School, and he has influential business identity around the world. Michael Porter is so famous that when I walk down the hallway to my office at Harvard Business School, and he says "Hi" to you in a way that makes you unhappy for a whole week. He's an amazing guy. And the thing that he gets known for is what is called the five forces frame. That's a very important concept that has application to the international relations arena. What the five forces framework is about is basically based on empirical research about profitability of business organs. It basically says the single most important determinant of profitability is not anything the CEO does, is not any decision about product, or anything like that. The single profitability determinant is do you happen to be upgraded in the industry, that is itself a very profitable industry for almost all benefits. You don't have to upgrade your leadership and it still goes pretty well, but the single important factor is being in a profitable industry, the second piece of the argument is what determines if an industry is profitable or not, certain structural features.

There are five forces. One of the five forces is the pattern of rivalry among industry competitors. And some industries have a pattern of rival of competition among the competitors. That is destructive for the profitability of the industry for everybody. And in that kind of industry, everybody loses, and it does not matter how good your leadership is, it does not matter, you are in a bad industry structure.

For example, if you are an industry and competition is so cutthroat that firms compete by lowering prices in order to take market share from competitors, lower prices even below their own costs. They are losing money. They hope temporarily in order to acquire greater market share, but the problem with that is that the behavior is reciprocated by the competitors. So it's very good for consumers—the prices go down, there is no good for any business. And they will never raise the prices because the competitors have lower competitive prices. That is an example on destructive rivalry with in an industry.

I think Mike Porter's 5 forces and particularly pattern rivalry give some very good insights into some of the challenges in international relations arena, what the great powers, I won't name (audience laugh), what the great powers need to do, is to figure out a better pattern of competition, there certainly would be competitions among the leading powers and cooperation. Competition is real, it's inevitable. But the challenge is how we form the pattern of competition andpattern of rivalries, which is not constructive, for the whole world and for everybody. So that's an arena in which I think everybody is interested in international relations, try to come up with new ideas about how we can better manage the process of competition.

Any people know Dr. Henry Kissinger? He was the Secretary of State with President Nixon when there was a famous relation breakthrough between China and the United States. One of the interesting things that Dr. Kissinger has said, famously, is thatthere's so few new ideas in policy in international relations because of how bureaucracy works.

In the United States, the president is the ultimate decision maker of foreign policy, but typically there is a process by which the different bureaucracies of the States Department and the Defense Department and etc. generate options for the president to make decision of. And as Dr. Kissinger put it: what typically happens is the president is given three options, only three options, the problem is that two of the options are so extremely as to be ridiculous, as Kissinger put it, one option is nuclear war, the other option is to surrender, and there is a third option which is the option that bureaucrats want. So when we put together the two ridiculous options that will never happen, and the option that bureaucrats want is almost always the perpetuation of the existing policy, so nothing changes, usually, and we got to do better than that, we need a process whereby more creative ideas of all sides be presented. And again this is not a challenge to anybody's leadership; every leader wants new ideas to consider. Different systems will sort out in different ways, whether the process is ultimately making the decisions. But everybody's job is to help in form that decision-making process with ideas as creative as possible.

Let me conclude this by giving you a couple of words of advice. First of all, don't ever run for class president unless you have something better to do without your ego, you need better motivation than that. But for more generally, I just believe, the best way to be, not just happy in a while, but also successful, is really to be focused on other people, as opposed toyourself much more often than focusing on yourself. I truly believe that that goes for every context you can think of, including when you write your application essays to Harvard Business School, they don't want to hear how great you are. They want to hear what have you done as a leader to make the lives of other people better, because that's the person the School wants to put a bet on.

Secondly, I want to emphasize that, trust yourself that the ideas you have are valuable. You should share your ideas, don't worry about the possibility that someone would say that's a ridiculous idea. Do your best to create a culture inwhich crazy ideas, not just me, but everybody else are welcome. It doesn't mean that the decision maker is going to adapt these ideas, but there is a value you are putting out there, really creative thoughts. Again, it doesn't mean any of them will win, but in some of the crazy thoughts, there is an element, this is really valuable.

The very last thing is, one good way I think, to improveyourself, is to regularly ask for, and listen to, and avoid reacting defensively to constructive feedback from other people. And it's one of the single best you can do today. Thank you so much for listening to me.

同感能力、创新和价值创造

AndyZelleke 哈佛大学商学院首席教授

此次由 AndyZelleke 先生带来的演讲的题目是“同感能力、创新和价值创造”。演讲前,Zelleke 先生与台下的听众展开了现场互动,进行了一次小调研:有多少同学打算将来经商;多少同学有意从政;若同时有两场旨在培养听众一流演讲能力和倾听能力的课程,同学们会如何选择。在对同学们的选择做出简要评述后,Zelleke 先生引出其“同感能力(empathy)”的演讲主题。

首先,Zelleke 先生通过讲述自己在哈佛商学院讲授领导力(leadership)和创造力(creativity)课程的经历,介绍了领导力的概念。结合自己参选大学班长的经历,Zelleke 先生与同学们分享了自己对领导力的三点理解:一、欲成为一位有领导力的领袖,初衷不应是为满足自身虚荣,而是为他人服务;二、领导力的本质在于将自身与所信仰的理念结合,并对他人产生影响;三、应当做服务型而非控制型的领袖。此外,Zelleke 先生还介绍了来自哈佛商学院的教授与学者们关于领导力的其他重要观点:例如身处高位并非领导力存在的必要条件,每个人都可以是潜在的领袖;领袖为身边环境创造并塑造一种文化等。随后, Zelleke 先生引入了创业精神(entrepreneurship)的概念。他指出,创业精神是一种不受当下资源限制和制约的、对潜在机遇的不懈追求。创业精神是一种在“变化”面前尤为显著的领导力。有创业精神的领袖不受制于眼前的蝇头小利,而是要发掘能够实现价值最大化的机遇。

其次,Zelleke 先生简要介绍了哈佛商学院的案例教学法,并指出哈佛商学院的使命是向学生提供实际的“领导力经历”(leadership experience)以培养学生的领导力。随后他举例讲述了自己运用“以人为中心的思维模式”(human-centered designed thinking)的同感能力教学方法以及在哈佛商学院开展一门实践课程的经历。

最后,Zelleke先生简要阐述了同感能力分别在商界尤其是产品和服务领域的创新,商业谈判以及国际关系和外交政策三大领域中所能起到的重要作用。

CHAPTER

Mr. Gama Perruci

玛瑞埃塔学院麦克唐纳领导力和商业中心主任

Dean of the McDonough Leadership Center, Marietta

Serving Society through Innovative Education: The McDonough Model of Undergraduate Leadership Development

The way that McDonough center was developed was in 1986 Bernard McDonough, the gentle man in the painting there, he passed away. He was a famous in dustrialist. When he passed away, the family wanted to honor him—he was a successful leader in the wanted to give the college 20 million dollars. The faculty met and they were divided into two camps. One camp said, "No! We don't do leadership. Leadership is for graduate programs, for the military. The military they have leadership development program. We are a liberal arts institution. Liberal arts institutions don't do leadership. Give back the gift." Another group said, "I'll take the money." So they had the meeting where they had to vote. Most faculty members approved to accept the gift. The founding dean took the statement by the faculty member, turned that around and made that the mission of the center. In English, the term "give back" has two meanings. One meaning is to return. So to say "give back the gift" is to "return the money".

The other meaning is to contribute, to give something that you have of value to society. So the founding dean took that statement which meant the first meaning and turned that to the second meaning. So the mission of the center is to bring, to take in the students, develop them and give them back to society with all the talents and skills developed. And then they get to live that mission of giving back. And that is our proposition of value. We want to develop innovative critical thinkers and problem solvers.

Now I'm thirsty. What should I do? Drink. How do I do that? I drink the bottle water here and problem solved. How does the water get here inside this bottle? A machine put the water in there and then somebody put it to the store and somebody bought it and brought it here and I drank it. How does the water get in the machine? From a river or from a lake. What if the water is contaminated in the river or in the lake? You have to purify. How do you do that? Some chemicals to treat the water. Then somebody has to do all of that to get to the point here. Now when you develop leaders, the leadership part is to get people to work together, to solve all of these challenges, to get to the point that now I'm thirsty and I drink the water. Does everybody in the world have this much easy access to water? Why is it that here in China, in Beijing, I got thirsty and I solved this in two seconds? Some parts of the world, to do that, it would take a big leadership solution to get all these parts that we talked about to work together. So if we want to do that, there are many areas that we try to develop so in the McDonough center we focused on these five areas to develop in the non-profit. We also offer several academic tracks so students can major in international leadership but most students do the minor or the certificate.

Now in terms of the model, to talk about the model then you have to talk about what we mean by leadership. When we and McDonough talk about leadership, then it's really a product of three branches. When we say leadership education, that's the knowledge part—the models and theories and ideas that we have developed over the centuries. There' s also leadership skill building and that is the training on developing the skills that would make you a more effective leader. So it' s not just to know the ideas but to know how to implement them, to have the skills to be an effective leader. Then the third is what we call leadership development. How you develop yourself into a better leader over time, because when you start, the challenges that you' re facing are very different from later on when you' re in a senior position. So the three areas become the comprehensive way to develop leadership. The model that we take is, each branch is one aspect of leadership development. The model is knowledge and then is combined with action and that leads to growth. So on the knowledge side, we offer four courses that are the basic knowledge that a leader should have.

Foundations of leadership. Organizational leadership. The third one is ideas being developed in this new century. The fourth is global leadership.

The action part, we talk about some ideas that you can take the students from the classroom and into the community. The combination of knowledge and action leads to growth and that is the wisdom part. When an experienced leader knows how to act, he certainly has the knowledge and experience. The frustrating thing in leadership is that there is no menu. So you have to learn from experience. You have to improvise, and when you improvise you make mistakes. Who loves to fail? But failure is good. You learn from the experience. So next time when you encounter something similar, you know how to act. And that' s how leaders grow. Leaders reflect. Leaders pay attention.

Now, back to the question of giving back the gift. We asked our students a very important question, "Leadership for what?" Because a lot of students think of leadership is for their own development, which is good, but it should be more than just you. So leadership is not about you. It is good to develop yourself but the real richness of leadership is when you help develop others and for the greater good. A lot of students have a hard time with that. Beyond graduating from the leadership program, we emphasize living the mission—go out there and do things. Students they start to live the mission, giving back the gift. We took students to New Orleans after the Hurricane Katrina, and they developed a project to help the community. So leadership for the greater good. And then we took a group of students with an IT, helping a school in Ghana. We brought computers and we set up a computer lab in this particular school. And then the IT person worked with the teachers. The students worked as substitute teachers.

We have a thousand graduates now and they are literally all over the world, doing all kinds of leadership challenges.

创新教育,服务社会
——麦克唐纳模式下的大学生领导力发展

GamaPerruci 玛瑞埃塔学院麦克唐纳领导力中心主任

在演讲的第一部分,GamaPerruci 先生就麦克唐纳领导力中心的历史背景做了简单介绍。领导力中心创立于 1986 年,目的是为纪念伟大实业家及成功的社区领导者麦克唐纳先生。其家族决定向大学提供两千万美元以启动大学生领导力发展的项目,而该校教员对于是否接受赠款意见不一。最终学校经过投票决定接受赠款,妥善利用并将成果回馈社会,进而确立了培养能够解决问题并具有批判性思维的创新型人才。

Perruci 先生在第二部分用“口渴了如何喝到水”的简单例子介绍了领导力在统筹某件事的不同步骤中所发挥的重要作用:瓶装水能解渴,而这之前的步骤包括河水净化、机器装瓶、商品上架、顾客购买。“喝水解渴”问题的最终解决需要将上述步骤进行统筹,这一过程是领导力的表现。为培养领导力,麦克唐纳中心专注五个领域,同时为学习国际领导力的学生提供学术课程。

据 Perruci 先生介绍,麦克唐纳模式下的大学生领导力发展有三个分支，分别是知识、领导技巧培养与领导力发展。三位一体形成综合培养领导力的途径，知行合一铸就成长即中心遵循的培养模式。

Perruci 先生表示，领导力的培养并没有说明书可以用来参考，可以从失败与经验中吸取教训。这样才能避免重蹈覆辙。优秀的领导者通过观察与反思获得成长。

最后，Perruci 先生做出总结，领导力的发展不是为了学生个人，而是为了帮助他人、提升自己并为了更多人的福祉。麦克唐纳中心鼓励学生走出去并身体力行，真正实现那笔捐款的价值，用培养出的领导力回馈社会。

CHAPTER 7

真家阳一

日本贸易振兴机构北京代表处负责人

Mr. Yoichi Maie

Japan External Trade Organization（JETRO）

Overseas Business Development of Japanese Companies and Utilization of Human Resources in Global Business

Good afternoon.

I' m Yoichi Maie, Deputy Director - General of JETRO Beijing Office. JETRO stands for the Japan External Trade Organization.

It' s a great honor for me to make a speech here in the University of International Relations, and I really appreciate for invitation from Ms. Hui Liu, Secretary of Party Committee, and Ms. Marie Li, Associate Professor of Center for International Strategy and Security Studies of UIR.

I' m not a native English speaker, and I' ve been staying in Beijing since last April and during this period, I had no opportunity to speak English.

So, it' s a hard challenge for me to make a speech in English, but I' ll try my best today.

Today my topic is "Overseas Business Development of Japanese Companies and Utilization of Human Resources in Global Business", but at first, taking this opportunity, I want to introduce my organization briefly.

JETRO is a Japanese government-related organization that works to promote mutual trade and investment between Japan and the rest of the world, just like CCPIT, China Council for the Promotion of International Trade in your county.

Originally established in 1958 to promote Japanese exports abroad, JETRO's core focus in the 21st century has shifted toward promoting foreign direct investment into Japan and helping small-to medium-size Japanese firms maximize their global export potential.

Outline of JETRO's overall sphere of activities are as follows.

1. Promoting foreign direct investment (FDI) into Japan

2. Promoting trade and business between Japan and the rest of the world

3. Assisting business expansion of developing countries

4. Contributing to trade policies and economic partnerships

As this part, JETRO provides information from surveys to research Today, I will explain about overseas business development of Japanese companies and utilization of human resources in global business by using the results of JETRO's FY2014 Survey on the International Operations of Japanese Firms.

Survey outline and profile of the respondent firms are as follows.

From December 2014 to January 2015, JETRO conducted a survey of Japanese firms with interest in business overseas.

The survey received valid replies from 2,995 firms (32.6% response rate), of which 2,334 were small-and medium-sized enterprises (SMEs) It covers topics including efforts of trade, overseas and domestic business development policies, business environments of emerging countries, globalization of management and so on.

In terms of export policy for the next three years or so, 78.6% of firms continued to express high motivation to expand exports from the previous year: 66.2% "intending to further expand exports" and 12.4% "expecting to launch exports".

By firm size, 75.3% of the large-scale firms said they intended to expand exports. AmongSMEs, thispercentagereached64.0%, andcombiningwiththe percentage who said they "intend to launch exports" (14.5%), it results in a total of 78.5%.

Regarding reasons for expanding exports, the most commonly cited reason remained "increasing overseas demand" (76.8%), while the percentage of "decreasing domestic demand" (50.4%) fell for the second consecutive year.

The percentage answering "higher profitability in overseas markets" (16.6%) rose over the same period.

When asked about future overseas expansion policies, the percentage answering "expand operations" was 56.7%, largely unchanged from the FY2013 survey (54.1%).

Although a majority of large-scale firms at 65.2% answered "expand operations," this percentage is lower than last year's (70.1%).

The percentage of large-scale firms giving this answer has shown a downward trend since FY2011, while the percentage answering "maintain the current scale" has increased.

On the other hand, the percentage of SMEs that answered "expand operations" has risen to 54.3% from last year's 50.2%.

Among companies that said they had policies of business expansion in the future, the top countries and regions which they reported as targets for business expansion overseas were China (56.5%), Thailand (44.0%), Indonesia (34.4%), the US (31.3%) and Vietnam (28.7%).

Many firms had policies of business expansion in other emerging markets as well, including India, Malaysia, the Philippines, Mexico and Myanmar.

31.3% of firms with policies of business expansion overseas choose the US for such expansion, up from 25.4% in the previous year. While the percentage among manufacturing firms (36.1%) is higher than among non-manufacturing firms (23.7%), both are up from last year.

Among countries and regions in Asia where respondents planned to expand their business, ASEAN6 (Singapore, Thailand, Malaysia, Indonesia, the Philippines, and Vietnam) was cited by 73.5% and China by 56.5%, as the ASEAN region has surpassed China for three consecutive years since 2012.

Appetite for expansion in ASEAN was high among both manufacturing (73.7%) and non-manufacturing firms (73.3%).

In China's case, the percentage choosing that country among manufacturing firms (58.7%) is down from last year (61.1%), while the percentage among non-manufacturing firms (53.2%) is up from last year (49.8%).

Among functions to be expanded overseas, the highest percentage of firms cited sales functions (82.9%), followed by production (general-purpose goods) (37.1%), production (high value-added goods) (29.2%), and R&D (change specifications for local market) (18.7%).

Both large-scale firms and SMEs had high levels of desire for expansion of sales functions. In addition, 30.9% of large-scale firms reported plans to expand regional HQ functions.

Regarding restructuring overseas and domestic bases and functions, the rate of cases of restructuring out of China increased to 27.8%, just below that of Japan with 49.1%.

As transfer destinations, ASEAN countries have continued to mark the highest at 47.9% of the all cases, having received 46.2% the year before.

By combinations of transfer sources and destinations, "transferring from Japan to ASEAN countries" (22.7%) and "transferring from China to ASEAN countries" (16.2%) made up notably large ratios.

Among respondents selecting "transferring from China to ASEAN countries", almost half of them (57 in 129 cases) selected Vietnam as the destination.

Transfers to Japan account for 7. 5% of all cases, which are mainly from China.

The most commonly cited reason for transfer of domestic and overseas bases was rising production and labor costs (41.0%).

The percentage citing that reason for relocation from China was 66.7%, even higher than last year's figure of 58.5%.

Regarding issues in the business environment in emerging countries, a lot of firms indicated labor-related matters as a concern in China and Thailand.

"Increased or increasing personnel costs" was commonly cited in China (48.8%), Thailand (29.1%) and Indonesia (21.2%).

The response rate of "labor shortage or difficulty in recruitment" was also relatively high in Thailand (18.6%) and China (14.4%).

"Inadequate infrastructure" was commonly cited in Myanmar (53.9%), Cambodia (44.9%), India (44.8%), Laos (38.7%), Vietnam (38.0%), Bangladesh (36.7%), and Indonesia (36.2%) among other countries.

On the other hand, China is relatively low (9.5%).

The top issue cited for China was "problems in protection of intellectual property rights" (52.6%), followed by "political risks or problems in social conditions and law and order" (49.8%).

From now, I'll speak about utilization of human resources in global business.

Regarding human resources strategies aimed at overseas business development, "fostering current Japanese employees to work effectively on the globalization of business" marked the highest at 45.1%, followed by "recruitment and promotion of foreign employees" (23.1%) and "mid-career recruitment of Japanese employees with deep knowledge of overseas business" (22.3%).

Higher percentages of SMEs than large-scale firms cited each of the strategies of "recruitment and promotion of foreign employees" (23.8%), "mid-career recruitment of Japanese employees with deep knowledge of overseas business" (23.8%), and "hiring of Japanese senior human resources (aged 60 and above) highly familiar with overseas business" (6.7%), indicating a focus on hiring human resources who can contribute immediately upon hiring.

The effort made most commonly by firms to train Japanese employees as global human resources was "enhancing English-language training in Japan" (21.4%), employed by roughly one-half of large-scale firms.

On the other hand, while only 17.1% of large-scale firms reported "no specific efforts implemented," this figure rose to 49.0% among SMEs, indicating that 49% of SMEs were making few specific efforts to train Japanese employees as global human resources.

The response rate of "currently hiring foreign employees" was 42.2%, with that of large-scale firms reaching 70.3% Although the rate of SMEs remained as low as 34.2%, they showed interests in recruitment of foreign employees, as can be seen in the percentage of those responding "not currently hiring foreign employees but expecting to consider recruitment of it" (23.8%).

A look at the employment status of foreign employees at the firms employing them, by position, shows that the highest percentage of 59.8% reported "general administrative staff includes one or more foreign employees". This figure was more than one-half among both large-scale firms (76.1%) and SMEs (50.3%).

Among firms that reported that they were "currently hiring foreign employees" or "expecting to consider recruitment of foreign employees," the highest percentage of 48.0% reported that they were hiring (or expecting to consider recruitment) foreign students studying in Japan.

Meanwhile, there is a gap between large scale firms (60.4%) and SMEs (43.2%) concerning the recruitment of foreign students studying in Japan.

While the most commonly used hiring method among large-scale firms was "openings announced by head office in Japan," among SMEs many respondents used employees' personal networks or the services of local governments or other public agencies.

Among firms that reported that they were hiring or employing foreign employees or considering doing so, together with "expanded sales channels" (41.0%) and "improved international negotiating ability" (39.7%), many firms recognized related benefits in improving the communication abilities of Japanese employees, for example through "improved language ability" (31.4%) and "lowering psychological barriers among Japanese employees in communication with foreign nationals" (27.9%).

By firm size, more large-scale firms (36.0%) than SMEs cited "strategic preparation for localization of management," while more SMEs (44.0%) than large-scale firms cited "expanded sales channels."

Frequently cited issues in hiring or employing foreign employees were "difficulty of sharing organizational vision" (18.5%), "numerous obstacles to communication with Japanese employees" (17.1%), and "high turnover rates since many foreign employees hope to return to their home countries or change employers in the future" (17.0%).

By firm size, more SMEs than large-scale firms cited "lack of understanding of methods of recruiting foreign employees" (8.6%) and "difficulty of procedures in Japan for working visas." (12.7%).

To develop overseas market, localization of corporate management is quite important.

I'll explain about the efforts for localization of corporate management of Japanese companies by using results of survey of Japanese-Affiliated Companies in Asia and Oceania (FY 2013 Survey).

Regarding "efforts for localization of corporate management ," the proportion of firms who responded "strengthen system to train or cultivate local human resources by focusing on localization of corporate management" (68.1%), and "assign local staff to a general manager or manager position" (51.3%) exceeded 50 %.

The proportion of large firms who responded "strengthen system to train or cultivate local human resources by focusing on localization of corporate management", "assign local staff to a general manager or manager position" and "reform personnel systems, such as a merit-based promotion system, by focusing on localization of corporate management" exceeded that of SMEs more than 10 points.

For "problems in promoting management localization", the highest percentage was marked at "lack of employee performance or employee awareness among local staff."

I want to enter the conclusion at here.

With the growing importance of the overseas market, SMEs are increasingly having to expand into other countries adapting to various local environments. These SMEs, however, often lack the global human resources necessary to do this.

In addition to foreign language ability, there are three core competencies required of global human resources:

(1) The ability to take decisive action.

(2) The ability to effectively convey oneself.

(3) The ability to succeed in a multicultural environment.

Large Japanese corporations are able to secure and foster global human resources through regular full-time employment of foreign workers, sending young workers still new to their respective fields abroad and conducting overseas executive training programs.

SMEs, however, find it much harder to take such measures and are hesitant to launch business operations overseas without such personnel.

In spite of this, there are some SMEs making efforts to expand abroad by independently securing the necessary human resources such as by utilizing foreign students in Japan, former trainees who completed special training courses for foreigners in Japan, Japanese with volunteer work experience overseas, or retirees.

To secure and foster global human resources, the government of Japan and related organizations have begun support efforts such as overseas internship programs.

For Japanese SMEs to develop business closely involved with global markets from this time forward, they should focus their energy on building people in addition to manufacturing products.

Support measures and tools for securing and fostering global human resources are as follows.

Overseas internship programs targeting young business people. Learning courses and seminars on overseas businesses Training courses for human resources abroad Support for global human resource development of the private sector Original training programs and projects organized by specialized organizations and universities with proven know-how on overseas dispatch of personnel and other personnel training.

Now, I finish my speech here.

Finally, I want to appreciate again for the invitation here in University of International Relations, thank you so much.

日本企业海外商业发展与全球化商业发展中人力资源的运用

真家阳一　日本贸易振兴机构北京代表处负责人

真家阳一先生首先对日本贸易振兴机构做了简单介绍:该机构是一个旨在促进日本与其他国家相互贸易和投资的政府组织,主要业务内容包括:一、促进外国直接投资;二、促进日本与其他国家的贸易;三、协助发展中国家的商业扩展;四、为贸易政策和经济合作伙伴做贡献(例如提供调查和研究所需的信息资料)。

接下来,真家阳一先生引用数据,详细介绍了日本企业海外商业发展与人力资源的现状:

日本企业海外商业发展方面:据日本贸易振兴机构成员公司近年财政年度的分析报告显示,成员公司中无论规模大小,有出口贸易战略计划并付诸实践的占了一半以上,其中绝大部分把海外市场指向亚洲各国,以中国和东盟六国为首。产业则集中在零售业、大宗商品生产、高附加值商品生产及研发方面。生产基地也逐渐流向东盟六国,一个很重要的原因是劳动力成本的提高和劳动力短缺。

人力资源方面:为应对今后全球化商业发展更为激烈的状况,日本需要的人才应具备三个重要素质,包括有决断力、有领导力以及能够胜任多元化的工作环境。为实现这一目的,日本政府组织和大型企业开展一系列活动帮助实现国际化人才战略,其中包括:为年轻的商业人员开展海外交流项目、开展海外商业活动教育课程、开展海外人力资源课程等。

CHAPTER

Ms. Chen Xiaojing Director

HR Business Partner for JVs

Current Requirements for Talents

Ladies and gentlemen, dear students, I am honored to have an opportunity to deliver a speech here and I would like to invite you to take a journey with me in the context of Asia and China. My presentation today will be divided into three parts, what do companies look for, what kind of programs do companies use to develop talents, and how to choose the right company and job that fits you.

Before I start, I would like to share my own working experience with you. At first, I worked in Volkswagen for about 18 months and learned a lot. Then in 1996, I started my own business and became a Chinese entrepreneur in Germany. Four years ago, I came back and started all over again as a business partner of Volkswagen in China.

The development of Volkswagen in China is not strange to everyone here in China. The cars we made in China actually are produced by joint ventures, which are not only strategic partners but also operational ones. In the structure of JV, the work of human resources is often charged by Chinese side. So far, there have been 700,000 employees behind these fine cars, which means that JV has been providing great opportunity to develop strong human resources group in China.

Well, let us go to the first part—talent identification.

Here is a chart of statistics about the situation of about 17,000,000 Chinese graduates finding jobs. And the number of students is predicted to decrease in the next 5 or 6 years. On the other hand, on newspapers, we often read many hot topics that companies are complaining about shortage of talents. Talents war is happening in our society, and many HRs are striving to attract many excellent people, including some who have overseas education background to come back to China and work with us. And we also heard that managers are feeling difficult to deal with the 90s generation and in order to solve this problem, the managers are receiving some training courses to learn to get along with the young generation. So here is the question: how can we put the large amount of graduates into the talent pool which is in the urgent need? This morning, we heard Ms Wang lectured about international leadership. However, from the perspective of company, we don't want a team full of leaders. We need members. It is very important to put the right person in the right place. It is the criteria that guide company to select candidates. The clear vision about your own strength and weakness can help you find a fit working place. Here is also a profile about the employees the international company want. I have asked my HR colleagues about which one among all the elements is the most important standard to value a person? They said that "never give up". Why? In china, we are facing the extreme fast development. Take Volkswagen as an instance. During the last four years, our company has opened many new factories in China. It started with Yizhou, and then followed by the Ningbo plant, Wulumuqi plant and Changsha Plant. That means we need huge amount of people who have bold spirit to achieve it.

Here are some company expectations for candidates. You should be highly qualified and motivated graduates and experienced professionals. Initially, you may feel scared by these conditions—multiskills and ability of doing everything.

But in the reality, it is very hard to become and find this sort of talents. Therefore, the advice from me is that focus on your strength, learn and improve yourself as much as possible in your college time.

After we know the situation in the job market, what kind of talents that companies want to hire, we come down to what measures that Chinese companies use to hire staff. If you focus on the tendency of development in the traditional job market, you will notice that social media has an increasingly important role in the current market. I also strongly recommend you to attend the job fair where you can have the chance to compare one company to another one. After using several channels, you might find ideal jobs and then go through the recruitment process including interviews and the tests posed by assessment center. Different companies must have slightly different requirements for candidates so that you need to have distinct preparations. If Volkswagen is the company you want to work in, you should know that the knowledge about cars is much needed. Another thing I want to say is about the development of candidates. In Volkswagen company, we also have many foreign employees, many of whom somehow can speak fluent Chinese. We can say the international atmosphere exists in working environment in China.

Then come to my second part—what can the international company provide or we can say what kind of platform the employees are standing at. Serving people is a very central value for Volkswagen, who represent customers, employees and even the whole society. As for the corporate value, what is the difference between the German and American companies in China? The first thing came up for me is punctuality. Time is absolutely very important. The other thing for me is expertise. In Germany, to be a engineer is a quite proud thing. And most managers in that country start from that position in that country. Personally, I believe America focuses more on business development mode while German counterparts much more focus on engineering to make the best product. Like Volkswagen, we offer many programs to improve employee's expertise. As a top employer, we invest in our employees and expect excellent performance. All the fruits that staff achieve are recognized and appreciated by the company. As a top employee, you are costumer-and service-oriented, and willing to spare no effort to do as much as you can. I firmly believe that the huge supply of graduates and the companies' demand of talents will sometime meet together. The whole world is open for you and you have the free choice and great opportunity to realize your own value. Honestly, I am very proud to be invited to talk on this stage and pass my personal experience to fellow students and encourage you embrace the future.

We come down to the third part and start with a question: has anyone of you tried to find a job in company? First, you need to figure out which kind of company is suitable for you. There are many channels available today, such as the company's official social media account, job fair. Then, it is very crucial to compare the training programs that different corporations provide. The following questions can be taken into your consideration. Do they have international working environment? What's their mode of getting along with employees? Do they help personal development? I will not go to details. But I hope you can have a healthy and cooperative relationship with your leaders. Win-win situation between two sides is the most ideal result.

To conclude, I hope you all can choose your own way forward. The tests and marks are not the only things you should attach great importance to in the college. Developing yourself in the all-round way is significant. Start now! Analyze your own strengths and weaknesses and move forward with the bold spirit. Best wishes.

Thank you!

当代人才需求

陈晓京　大众(中国)投资有限公司人力资源主管

陈晓京女士的演讲主要分为三个部分:公司需要怎样的人才,公司如何培养、发展员工,以及作为求职者,怎样才能找到适合自己的岗位和公司。

陈晓京女士首先与听众分享了自己的职业经历。最初在德国大众有限公司18个月的工作经历为其之后在德国创业奠定了坚实的基础,她也成为了在德国的中国创业人。四年前,陈晓京女士回国并成为大众有限公司的人力资源总监。作为一家合资企业,大众公司的人才招聘和选择权主要由中方做主,这对于构建优良人力资源队伍,支持大众在华发展是一次重要机会。

随后,陈晓京女士给出了对于人才的合适定义:从图表和调查来看,如今中国的毕业生数量一直在增加;而另一方面,企业人才短缺的话题也常常见诸报端,公司之间也存在人才战争。如何将大批毕业生与公司人才需求相结合成为非常重要的议题。此外,陈晓京女士选取了独特的视角并结合其对于领导力的看法,对该议题进行了解读:公司需要的是将人放在合适的岗位上,然后以团队为单位,团结协作。领导力很重要,但公司更应该看重员工自身的优势,使之在合适的位置上发挥出最大潜能。跨国公司更倾向于有专业素养、跨文化竞争力、掌握多语言的人才。当然最重要的一点就是,永不放弃。不放弃的思维会让员工有更强的解决问题的能力。中国正在快速发展,而这种发展需要大量的人才去推动。

接着,陈晓京女士介绍了跨国公司为人才提供的良好平台,包括多元的工作环境和一流的国际团队,还有针对个人制定的一些长期发展计划等。但不同国家的企业会有所不同,比如德国公司更注重技术发展,而美国则更看重商业的拓展。

对于求职者最关心的问题,陈晓京女士也给出了自己的看法:在中国这样一个大市场中如何选择公司？她一直鼓励大家参加企业招聘会或通过新媒介关注动态。在求职前和求职过程中，要做好事先的调查，在企业之间进行对比，最后结合自身情况。在公司的培训项目中，也能从企业不同部门获得许多经验。当今世界为人们提供了许多选择。合适与否、雇佣者与被雇佣者之间的理念关系是否平衡非常重要。老板与员工之间的双赢才是理想的结果。

最后，陈晓京女士表示希望当代大学生能够跟随时代、了解自身，不放弃、脚踏实地走自己的路。

CHAPTER

Mr. Hanshi

清华大学卡内基全球政策研究中心研究员

Resident Scholar Carnegie–Tsinghua Center for Global

Current Situation of Global Business

Thank you for coming to the conference on the Saturday afternoon. And I hope it doesn't mean anything funny to you. It seems to suggest that what I have is mine and what you have is also mine. Your secret is not secret to me. I am not talking about trade secret or commercial espionage. Let me give you a quick comment on what is happening in the business world in general. First of all, one should have a basic understanding of the concept of "reshoring". America now is against the policy of offshoring. Obama wants to bring back the manufacturing industry, so "reshoring" is advocated. "Reshoring" is a bold concept but it is not happening. Two big companies make big deals about reshoring, one is General Electricity, and one is Apple. GE hires workers in the States, but they may quit because manufacturing jobs are noisy, dirty and can be physically dangerous and the factory is in trouble. Apple brings small factories back to USA and makes iPhone against its tiny investment. I ask another question to keep your attention. Does anyone in the room doesn't know the name of Foxconn Company? And do you know the Chinese gentleman by the name of GUO Taiming? What is really happening to the Apple Company is that its manufacturing contractor is still in

Taiwan. It's a big deal. Thus the US's restoring policy of bringing back the manufacturing industry is still not a reality. Another interesting thing is about the US. It is doing something in the manufacturing field somehow. Germany makes the BMW in South Carolina and makes a lot of BMW SUV exported around the world. China's market makes millions of dollars that makes it the biggest export. And this is somehow in contrast with the restoring, where you can still use the high-income countries as low-cost manufacturing base and export rather sophisticated products to other countries. Just keep in mind the BMW from Carolina to China, its price soared twice. China's export still goes strong. In the investment part, I have to say that China's export still goes strong, and what we hear in the newspaper and on radio is that it is still great and cultivates domestic market. I want to say that is not the reality. If you look at the export data, the gap between USA and China is still large. Exports of the devices are no longer made in coastal areas like Zhuhai, Shenzhen, but in the inner land like Foxconn in Zhengzhou. Millions of Chinese people now work in its production and export-related jobs. And the working places are no longer in coastal areas like Shenzhen anymore but in inland cities like Xi'an, Chongqing. Last but not least is that, Chinese export to Vietnam is really staggering and specific things like steel to Vietnam, you will wonder if Chinese export still goes strong. I will suggest you to take a look at Chinese output of fertilizer to India which went up in first quarter. So what media is not telling you is that not only China makes export to high-income countries like before, but also in a way to Southeastern Asia like what Japan and South Korea did to China decades ago. I am really talking business activities within the boundary of a corporation. It becomes separable and dispersed around globally. Assembly can be made in somewhere like Thailand. Speaking of being creative, this is what MIT professors did back into the 1960s using a bit of micro economy. Well not, I think there shall be some economics classes in the University of International Relations. Because it is a very useful tool if you have a lot of things that would be inexpensive. Conversely, if you have a few, it's rather expensive. In the case of capital, in DC referring to developed countries. You may have quite a lot capital with lower costs compared with high-income countries. In there, for the same costs you will have minor usage of labor. The poor countries, the less developed ones, let's do capital researching surveys in Canada and the United States where capital are greatly required. Something next to agriculture requires human proficiency which is kept in areas like Hong Kong, Taiwan and South Korea. All these activities basically are either in house, in domestic areas through commanding contracture or on the market where negotiations are possible and products are traded on prices. So what is the major difference? Between these two, the quickest finding is that you will not agree to someone that gives you an order, while in the first one, within the hierarchy of the company, activities are inter-created. They will wonder why I have to do something like that. On the case of boss, it is because I told you so. You have to do it to your suppliers or customers. You cannot sit down and negotiate for a price. All right, now usually the manager makes decisions about the activities we mention especially that around the globe. Get things down through a contractive process. This is NBA's main trick. We list down two factors that keep you doing what you should have done. For managers, some will do things just by themselves because they are better than anyone and extremely important to them. But when somebody in the market place do a better job, for example, how about you need a mop to clean the floor, you don't have to make a company of it, so you buy it. The strategic importance to you is done to relative strength of what we do. We can list more factors that affect you and can help you make a decision. Innovation and creation.

Since we are talking about innovation and creation, I will say two American economists that are awarded with Nobel Prize on one of these items. They say people can be speculative and opportunistic in domestic politics. You may be threatened, blackmailed if you do not do things. Nobody likes it but somehow it happens again. Suppose a supplier makes products for his customers, a very complicated product that requires certain investment. Several purchase orders are made then the supplier wants to increase the price. This is when the customer starts to blackmail, because a rather specific investment for a complicated product creates transaction cost. In business relationships, what you want to do is to keep the cost down. Let's look at the contract manufacturer Foxconn Company and all sorts of made-in-chain categories and see how the consideration of supply helps us understand which of these organizational arrangements we would accept in contract. At the bottom of the list is through negotiations of parties where you are told so. In the department store of the US, you display your products either form promotion or regular sales. It would be that your pay changes over time. You have Chicago companies through generations supplying to one of the largest department chains in the US. Secondly, two parties, customers and suppliers can work together and thirdly, about transaction costs. We can arrive on organizational arrangements that keep us from doing frightening things. In this case, business is rather simple. For any supplier nearly qualified to be rather flexible in common design that they are willing to accept or make investment to please customers, it cares a lot whether the company is serious enough. In terms of government structure, the owner of a business really did not think it through. It has the notion that you have to do everything that is within your responsibility. So he did not care much about others, just a simple product and controlled quality. A New Jersey company wants to bring PVC products from China, with the condition that PVC should be more than necessary. It is the particular case when a company can make products with limited sourcing and mechanism quality control by a third party. So more complicated, one of two major brands in its categories of candle products that it switches supplier from Mexico to China and also it is done at the head of others. Here we help locate a factory not in coastal China but in inland. Coastal companies are moving in themselves. Last one about product when you are involved in industrial activities, the company sets up a sourcing center of their own so as to sell products under the same brand.

So in summary, we can see some regularity that you can use in China to help. Most complicated, mechanical devices, IT products, high-end customers, virtually approach in place where you can do so through strategic lines. Some companies now change their supplier chain and develop customers with a company in reverse.

全球商业现况

韩实　清华大学卡内基全球政策研究中心研究员

韩实先生首先就全球制造业现状做了简单介绍：目前美国制造业的商业形式为离岸外包，但总统奥巴马希望能实现企业回流。但美国两大企业通用电气公司和苹果公司都未能实现回流预期。但与此同时，美国仍然是复杂产品的低成本生产基地，宝马系列产品和斯帕坦堡模型就是典型的例子，这说明高收入国家也会得到更多的投资。同时，中国出口依然强劲，产品组件出口韩国，郑州设有 iPhone 产品组装公司，服装外包商业出口越南等东南亚国家。而现今全球商业公司的另一个特征就是公司内各项业务活动都在全球范围内分散开来独立进行。

随后，韩实先生介绍了商业运作的主要方式，包括两部分：一是商业公司等级制度及内部活动的直接整合，通过计划和协调、指挥和控制以及行政管理进行。二是市场业务关系，由公司独立决定，自愿交换和市场价格也发挥重要作用。

提到小公司，韩实先生表示，其价值链重构需要频繁的设计变更和由第三方进行的质量控制。对于其战略协调性，要更加关注灵活性和客户服务。管理结构方面需要详细的供货协议、指定供应商以及无购买数量的承诺。

对于中型企业,其产业链重构需要在关键组件、密封保密、无工厂参观方面的调整。中型企业的战略协调性在于样品测试。而其管理结构则体现在订单采购和保证无购买量上。而对于中端市场的品牌公司来说,其产业链重构需注意多产品和人身安全问题。在战略协调性方面,需着重于技术能力和知识产权保护。而在管理结构上则要注意国外分公司和国内采购中心。

CHAPTER 10

Mr. Michael Milone

Heinz 集团前执行副总裁

Heinz former executive vice president

Creation and Leadership

It is my pleasure to be here. I used to travel to China once every three or four months. But I haven't been back for 6 years. Now I have noticed a few changes, especially the size of the airport. It has expanded quite a bit. One of the main things I will talk about is the executive residence project. I am gonna cover innovation and leadership.

The title of the Project was "How will the world be different in 2040?" A lot of students thought this would be a series of lectures about technology which was sadly mistaken. I am not a scientist, though I did study and obtain a BA in Biochemistry when I went to college. My objectives for the project were to help the students get more out of their liberal arts degree by developing an intellectual curiosity and awareness of the world around them. Specifically there is a tremendous amount of information that is out there and easily available if you just open your eyes a little and take some time to observe and wonder. I always wished I had more time for this kind of reflection and this was an opportunity for me to do the same. I actually learned along with the students. It was a real opportunity to develop critical thinking as well as gain some specific knowledge. I sometimes refer to the students that this was an exercise in learning how to participate in a party.

The students really struggled at first because of the lack of structure. While the students could handle an assignment like, "Bring a 10-page paper on Subject X to class", they could not handle "Come to class ready to discuss ideas and how you think the future might look." We spent a good deal of time expanding and talking about the breadth of possibilities out there, then contracting and focusing on more narrow subjects. I had some unique assignments for them, for example, one of these assignments was to watch the movie called Back to the Future. And particularly Back to the Future 2 talks about time traveling from 1990 to 2015. So by looking at that movie, students could look at what 25 years ago people thought today would look like. Another interesting assignment was over winter break; I asked all the students to take time sitting around the dinner table with their families and friends and asked people what their view of the future would look like.

Interestingly, I divided the 9 participating students into three groups and they independently all decided to focus on communications, probably since cell phones and media are such a constant part of their everyday lives. I would say we succeeded against my objectives and definitely had fun.

I am going to talk about my observations and hypotheses about innovation and leadership based upon 32 years of senior marketing and international business experience. These are my thoughts and hypotheses, not necessarily absolute truths. I am going to build this presentation around 2 key points. First, the long-term health and sustainability of an enterprise requires innovation; two, innovation requires leadership.

To begin making the first point, I want to pose a question. Who would each of you say are the great non-political visionaries of our time? Who are the individuals, living or dead, who have had the biggest influence on our everyday lives, today? My nominations would be Walt Disney, Steve Jobs and Elon Musk. The thing all of these folks have in common is they are all acknowledged leaders and innovators.

I would like to further build on my point, "innovation is required for the long-term health and sustainability", by discussing a few business axioms you have probably heard in some forms or another.

- If it is not broken, don't break it.

- If it is not broken, break it.

- If you keep doing what you have been doing and expect a different result, that is the definition of insanity.

I ascribe to the second two, and not the first. It is inevitable in business or in everyday life that competition will challenge you and you need to adjust. Let me relate a few personal experiences that illustrate my point of view.

One of my earliest assignments when I went to work at Heinz was to update and document the history of Heinz's Ketchup. This was something that was done periodically; at least it was back then, to memorialize our successes and failures, to learn from what we have done right and what we could have done better. At that time, Heinz had about a 40% share of the US retail market. Heinz was recognized as the clear leader and was just about the only ketchup that could be found in restaurants with a share of about 90%. The first thing I learned that shocked me was in 1960, just 20 years prior, Heinz only had about a 23% share, equal to 2 other brands, so the leadership position was built fairly quickly. Most important and to the point, this growth was not a smooth, steady line upward, rather it was a series of steps and plateaus, with each step being traced to a specific innovation. Now I take a very broad view of innovation. Some of these steps were advertising campaigns, others were new package sizes, and still others were promotions. I find that often young business folks are hesitant to change or take risks and think their job is fine tuning, particularly in marketing.

My belief, and what I preach is big ideas lead to big gains, and we are all looking for big gains.

Here is another example using a relatively small innovation. Heinz Home-style Gravy was the first product that I was given to manage as the product manager. It was a fairly new product and had been struggling because any woman worth her sort of knew how to make gravy, and buying prepared gravy was beneath most housewives. Due to some convoluted regulations and incorrect interpretation of them by our labeling overseers, Heinz beef-flavored gravy was called brown gravy. I still remember the advertising agency saying, "brown is a color, not a flavor! This is something we have to fix." To keep the story short, I was first told they were mislabeling, and then I forced the internal regulators to go over the details with me and our product developers. It turned out that all we needed to do was stop the process for a second and call an inspector over to see an intermediate product that we called our beef stock.

One of the biggest steps on the ketchup chart is the introduction of the plastic ketchup bottle. There was one small problem. Ketchup turns brown in the presence of oxygen. This is why you sometimes get a brownish ring around the top of the bottle. And plastic at the time was permeable to oxygen. So launching this package required the development of a new technology, the layering of different types of plastic to create an oxygen barrier. Not only that, the start-up posed tremendous challenges. Ketchup is filled into the bottle hot. Plastic changes shape with heat, so we had an object of changing shape moving down the production line. Little things like the glue to keep the labels on had to be modified to be less brittle. So this was a major technological innovation.

But the really remarkable part of this story is that we just beat competition. The development and launch was a hotly debated topic within the company. The new bottle was more costly and carried lower margins. Further, we did lots of research which showed clear consumer interest. The bottle we tested would achieve about an 8% share. But what would happen if a competitor launched the plastic bottle? Again, the result was about an 8% share, but in this situation, Heinz lost all 8 share points. The rest is history. We launched, and within 6 months, 40% of our business was in plastic. We later learned that two weeks after we struck an exclusive supply agreement with our bottle manufacturer, our main competitor approached this supplier asking for an exclusive arrangement. About 5 years later, 100% of the category shifted to plastic packaging.

Moving to my second point, innovation requires leadership. Innovation requires funding, direction, prioritization, encouragement, among a host of other things. Most of all, it requires support and commitment from the top. Innovation cannot be legislated. A CEO cannot pound on the table or jump up and down and hold his breath until he turns red in the face and expects to get innovation. The right atmosphere and organizational enthusiasm are required, and these require strong, positive leadership and support from the top.

It often starts with a strong R&D program and funding, but successful R&D requires leadership. I am not talking about brilliant scientists. Early on when I was a new business unit leader, we were all asked to come to the meeting first with our "secret dream", then the next year with our "unthinkable thought". Well, as you might expect, this generated a good degree of eye rolling and jokes. But in retrospect, this exercise and taking it seriously was a critical factor in the success of my business, and ultimately, my career. The secret dream I presented one year was to have a lower price for canned cat food than my competitors. We held a slight premium price, but new competitors were pressuring the whole market, including ourselves with low pricing. For 5 straight years, we had tried to take a price increase, only to be forced to roll it back. So we thought, "If competition won't let us increase prices, how about if we price not equal to them, but below them?" This would of course destroy the economics of the business and category. But about the same time, I stumbled across an article and concept called price-based costing. A traditional approach to pricing is cost-based pricing…take your costs, add your expected margin and that is what you need to set as your price. With price-based costing, you turn this model on its head. First, ask what you want the price to be, then allow for your expected or desired margin, and determine what your cost must be. Finally, you must then engineer your product design and costs to hit this target. This simple, but radical and innovative way of thinking turned the industry on its ear.

Another enabler of innovation is outsourcing. Lots of folks believe that all innovation must come from R&D. However, it is impossible for anyone company or enterprise to have all possible and needed capabilities. Therefore, outsourcing is a logical solution. Heinz relied very heavily on our suppliers, particularly packaging suppliers, and on associations with universities.

All of these innovation enablers, which are not by any means meant to be all inclusive, require leadership and support from the top. All of these programs require leaders to foster, identify, motivate, and conduct and also to implement innovation.

Onefinalthoughtoninnovationandleadership. Becauseofmybroad international business experience, culture and business is something I am frequently asked to talk about. My observation is that linear-active cultures, which are heavily western, tend to be more innovative than reactive cultures, which tend to be more eastern. This is not surprising to me, since eastern cultures tend to have a much richer and longer history, and therefore tie to the past. As eastern cultures grow and learn to become more independent as individuals and innovate, watch out for how countries like China can transform the world. And I am not talking about economic or population power, I am talking about the power of innovation and impact on leadership of the world.

And with that thought, I think it is appropriate to end with a reminder of my two main points. 1) The long term sustainability of an enterprise requires innovation; and 2) Innovation requires leadership.

创新与领导力

MichaelMilone Heinz 集团前执行副总裁

MikeMilone 先生的发言包括两个重点:一是企业的健康与持续发展需要创新,二是创新需要领导力。

在演讲的前半部分,Milone 先生结合自身经历讲述了创新对于企业的重要性。在商业社会或日常生活中,人们都会遇到竞争。在理想状态下,我们应当用创新来应对挑战。1960 年 Milone 先生刚加入亨氏集团时,集团的市场份额仅为 23%,二十年后已增长到 40%。每一次市场份额的大幅度提升都归功于大胆创新,包括新的广告、新的包装等。Milone 先生还列举了另外一些典型的例子,如把产品名"棕色肉汁"改为"牛肉肉汁",以及亨氏改进技术,把装番茄酱的容器换成塑料瓶。这些措施都是极大的创新,也使公司获得了巨大的成功。

之后,Milone 先生分享了自己对于创新与领导力的关系的观点:创新需要经费、氛围、指导方向、激励机制等,而这些都需要积极有力的领导。创新无法通过立法来实现,需要通过不同的方式与策略来促进。创新不仅来自研发,还可以来自业务外包。亨氏集团十分依赖供应商,而供应商在创新方面也起了很大的作用。另一种形式的创新是向其他企业或其他国家借鉴经验。但这种形式存在资源利用方面的弊端。这些创新方式都需要领导者来主导、识别、鼓励与执行。

最后,Milone 先生根据自己多年跨国从商经验做出总结,在他看来,西方文化比东方文化更能推动创新,但如今东方的国家也正迎头赶上,成为创新及领导世界进程中不容忽视的力量。

CHAPTER 11

Ms. Weidan

澳门大学法学院教授

Professor of Law, University of Macau.

Innovative Education to Nurture the Best Minds: Vision, Passion and Dedication

The economic globalization has become the catalyst for re-ordering and restructuring international relations in the twenty-first century. It requires our new conceptualization for global governance. The key issue of global governance is to improve the current international system from the one dominated by major powers to a more democratized system where emerging countries hold a stronger voice. Global governance aims to reform the international organizations, enhance the regulations for global problems and achieve a more balanced way for the distribution of growth between those countries who lead and other countries who lag.

Emerging economies such as BRICS (Brazil, China, India, Russia and South Africa) have provoked global attention and have been increasingly at the center of international negotiations, namely, the reform of international financial system, the reform of world trade system, the climate changes and so forth. Over the last two decades, Brazil, India and China have each undertaken market opening and have become deeply integrated into the world economy. Precisely because the emerging countries are important economic powers—they have become increasingly attractive markets. Since 2000, these countries have begun to move from a model of globalization primarily based on inbound investments, to one in which companies based in these countries are also significant sources of outward investment.

The building of a new political economy for a global society demands for internationally-minded talents, and in particular, the top talents from the emerging economies who have deep understanding of local cultures and are enthusiastic to apply creative solutions to the global problems.

Today, I am very honored to be able to participate in the 2nd Summer Palace Forum and to meet many promising students of the University of International Relations who will be engaged in international exchanges and cooperation after graduation, and perhaps some of you will be very lucky to work in international organizations and participate in the process of global governance. In this sense, the theme of this conference concerning cultivation and development for international organizations seems very appropriate. The title of my speech is "Innovative Education to Nurture the Best Minds: Vision, Passion and Dedication". I will divide my talk into three parts. First of all, I would like to share my personal views on a few key requirements of the best talents. In the second part, I will highlight some key points for innovative education aiming to nurture manpower, sharing some experiences of my home university: University of Macau. Finally, I will try to draw some conclusions of my talk.

Ⅰ. A global citizen: vision, passion and dedication

In our global society, top talents must be noble global citizens with high integrity and good personalities. In my personal view, in order to create values and make contribution for the global society in the future, young students have to bear in mind the following key prerequisites in their path of growth.

The first prerequisite is to have a global vision. Just like a driver who must know the destination and the direction before he or she starts the engine of a car, young students should have courage to dream and to think big. A man with dreams can be persistent and hard-working. Beautiful dreams in the young minds can help them achieve their maximum potential. To dream is a part of youth. Our lives would be very boring if we do not have dreams. Dreaming is a starting point for our life. Universities are a breeder or a cradle for young minds to dream.

Chinese young people are indeed very lucky fellows in our era. China's unique pathway in quest for a new identity in the era of globalization and its accelerated participation in the global governance have created many opportunities for Chinese youth to show their abilities and competitiveness. China is currently the world's largest holder of foreign exchange reserves. Since 2010, China has overtaken Japan as the world's second-largest economy. In 2013, China surpassed the U.S. to become the world's biggest trading nation. So far, China has acceded more than one hundred inter-governmental organizations and is a signatory member of more than three hundred international conventions and treaties. More and more Chinese people having served or are still playing important roles in international organizations. Just to name a few, Judge Shi Jiongyong, former President of International Court of Justice, Ambassador Wu Jianmin, former president of the International Exhibition Bureau, Ambassdor Sha Zukang, former head of the United Nations Department of Economic and Social Affairs, Professor Justin Lin Yifu, former Senior Vice President of the World Bank, Economist Zhu Min, Deputy Managing Director of International Monetary Fund, Economist Jin Liqun, Secretary General of the Interim Multilateral of the Asian Infrastructure Investment Bank, etc. They are all excellent examples for young students.

Certainly, having big dreams is not enough for one to achieve remarkable success later. The second prerequisite I would like to emphasize is passion, passion for knowledge, passion for self-improvement, passion for innovation and passion for life. The best students are often passionate to stick to their dreams and will not easily give up. The students should be courageous enough to be losers and to start afresh.

The third key prerequisite is dedication. A person called Leonard Swidler published Universal Declaration of a Global Ethic some years ago, "Those who hold responsibility for others are obliged to help those for whom they hold no responsibility. In addition, the Golden Rule implies: if we were in serious difficulty wherein we could not help ourselves, we would want those who could help us to do so, even if they held no responsibility for us; therefore we should help others in serious difficulty who cannot help themselves, even though we hold no responsibility for them". The talented students should know very well why they learn professional expertise and how to build a bridge between theories and practices.

Sooner or later, students will graduate from the university. Some may start their careers making use of their professional expertise learnt at the university, other may engage in different areas or fields. No matter what professions are chosen by them, they must be instilled to have various traits, in particular, a sense of responsibility and a spirit of dedication to the community. Young people have spent their best time in life in the university to learn not only professional expertise, but more importantly, a sense of responsibility and a sense of dedication to the nation, to the society and to the country, who can live with passion and lead with compassion. It is important for young people to know it is necessary to sacrifice oneself for the good of a large number of people and for the sake of the well-being of society ("greater good").

Ⅱ. Mission to nurture the best minds through innovative education.

We live in an era that everybody can learn from everywhere. Unlike old times, nowadays, professional expertise is not the monopoly of universities and universities are not the only places that the students can obtain their professional knowledge. However, I would rather consider that universities are still the best place for young people to build their personalities.

I talked about how to be become qualified talents who have vision, passion and dedication to succeed in the global environment and serve our nation in the future. In fact, vision, passion and dedication are equally applicable to university teachers. A teacher's role is to serve as a modest spur to induce the students to come forward with his or her valuable contributions. In ancient times of China, Han Yu once wrote a great piece on the mission of a teacher. "A teacher is to teach us the fundamental relationship between oneself and the society, the knowledge and skills to live in the society and to help us answer doubts in the learning process in our life". According to my understanding, a teacher not only points out for the students a direction, but also teaches the methods, techniques and skills. When the students encounter difficulties in their own practices, a teacher gives a hand and advice. When indicating a direction, a teacher teaches the students a way of thinking, professional knowledge and an attitude towards life. In our daily contacts with our students, we just simply open a subject for discussion and reflection and try to explore our students' potentials. As like a famous Chinese saying put it, "to throw away a brick in order to get a gem". Our final goal is that our students can surpass us and excel us. Personally I believe this is the true meaning of a teacher's career. A teacher's mission is to nurture the best students, and thereby he or she can fulfill his or her own ideal. Confucius taught us, "Now the man of perfect virtue, wishing to be established himself, seeks also to establish others." That is to say, the virtuous not only strive after lofty achievements themselves, but also try to help others do the same. In Chinese, it says "己立立人,己达达人"。

It is very noteworthy for teachers to not just teach but also stimulate. In this sense, a teacher and a student are like good friends in scholarly pursuit who learn from each other and cheer each other on. A teacher is more experienced than a student in the learning process and therefore it is very important for the teacher to motivate the students to find their potentials and strengths. Young people are potential persons. However, more easily, they can feel frustrated when their dreams got tossed and blown. A teacher's role is to accompany them with patience, care and love and let them know that they will never walk alone.

Once the students have set up their life goals and directions, a teacher cannot forget to develop fine qualities of his or her students. We all know that our habit was formed when we were young. We first make our habit, and then our habit makes us for the whole life. In this sense, young people need to some extent strict discipline to form a good character. Our life journey is full of failures and failures teach successes.

Easier said than done. The implementation of traditional education values requires innovative approach. In our rapid changing world of today, how education needs be modernized in order to achieve satisfactory results and ensure the teaching effectiveness? What are the ideal places to develop a close and regular contact with students and offer personal counseling? Please allow me to talk a little about my university's efforts and experiences.

The University of Macau has been ranked No. 40 in the Times Higher Education (THE) Asia University Rankings 2015. This is the first time the University of Macau has been ranked among the top 100 Asian Universities. Along these years, the university management has promoted actively a strategy of internationalization. The students have opportunities to meet the academic staff who come from different parts of the world with multi-linguistic and multi-cultural backgrounds. The humanities and language arts are developing together with natural sciences majors. In the curriculum designing, new knowledge of other disciplines has been offered from a whole-person development perspective. Considering the small economic scale of Macau and its narrow base of tourism and gaming industries, our university has been keeping offering academic training to prepare our students for global opportunities and transformation, and at the same time encouraging our students to think globally.

Currently, our university is launching a new "4-in-1" education model, which aims to implement whole-person education through the combination of discipline-specific education, general education, research and internship education and community and peer education, which are all integrated into the undergraduate curriculum for any discipline. I couldn't agree more with this new initiative. I think this innovative approach is in line with the great idea of "connection of theory and practice" developed by a famous Chinese philosopher Wang Yangming. Our priority is to help our students become people of action, people with wisdom and compassion, people who can make contribution to our society.

Following the example of world class universities, our university introduced a residential college system. All first-year undergraduate students from different backgrounds, majors and cultures are placed in residential colleges to experience communal living. There are in total 8 residential colleges that have been established. With distinct characteristics, all residential colleges have the same objective of nurturing future leaders. Many distinguished scholars and social elites worldwide are invited to talk and meet with the students living at the residential colleges. It is mandatory that each teacher and each student participate in at least two activities per semester. Through the residential system, the students are able to learn from the elites, the teachers and from their friends with different majors. More importantly, they can be trained to develop a sense of responsibility to respect others and to care for the community.

In addition to the activities organized by the residential colleges, the University of Macau has also adopted a mentoring system where each undergraduate student can be guided by his or her own mentor, who is usually a teacher of his major nominated by the University, about any problems related to learning, university life and career development plans.

Our university has also established close partnerships with private sector to offer interns and recruitment opportunities for graduates. The Bank of China is a good example. Around 10% of the workforce of Bank of China in Macau has graduated from the University of Macau. Recently, the Bank of China wanted to connect Chinese enterprises with Portuguese-speaking countries such as Brazil, Portugal, Angola and so on, and therefore created a platform for business in these countries. The Bank benefited from the Linguistic Department of our university in this project. The students majoring in Portuguese Language gained opportunities to apply their linguistic knowledge and at the same time they have been able to create more values for Chinese enterprises' investment activities in the Portuguese-speaking countries.

Ⅲ. Concluding remarks

While in defining the key goals of outstanding talents who are qualified to participate in the international dialogues and cooperation, many people would emphasize the high-level of academic credentials, inter-disciplinary professional knowledge and proficiency in foreign languages. These points are all true. However, in my view, the top talents must firstly be persons with high integrity and noble personality, who have vision, passion and dedication. I believe these features are highly important for the perseverance in pursing truth and justice and their love for their own country, for their nation and for the friendship and peace of the world. The young people must be confident and optimistic about our future and the future of the world. As long as the young people aim higher to devote themselves in serving for our society, they will have strong motivations to gain persistently knowledge and professional skills.

The mission of all universities for the sustained social development of our global society is to nurture the best young minds.

China plays a key role in the international community and takes more and more responsibilities on the world stage. It is deemed as the engine of growth or as a new force for economic development in Asia, and even for the rest of the world, after the global financial crisis. As China goes global, she will be engaged in ever more interaction with the world. On one hand, Chinese government is actively participating in the formulating of international regimes and global governance, on the other hand, more and more Chinese enterprises are investing overseas. Both the Chinese government and the private sector in China need a great number of talents who are highly qualified and competitive to create values and to serve for the community and society.

Therefore, universities must play a pro-active role and maintain close cooperation with the government and the private sector. It is ideally to create a triangle close interaction among academia, governmental body and private sector. In this way, the universities can offer better opportunities and favorable conditions for the young students to gain experience and to grow constantly.

培养出色人才的创新教育：视野、激情和奉献精神

魏丹　澳门大学法学院教授

魏丹女士在演讲一开始便指出，一个世界公民要有事业、激情和奉献精神。要想成为一个在世界化社会中能创造出价值的人，先决条件是要有国际化的视野。中国有其独特的世界化道路，这为当今中国的年轻人提供了很多机会。年轻人首先要有远大的梦想，这样才会有实现梦想的机会。其次是激情，年轻人要有激情，不惧失败才能坚持不懈。第三个必备的条件是奉献精神，学生们应当充分利用他们所学到的专业知识，用于实践、帮助他人。对社会和国家的责任和奉献精神是一个学生在大学最应该学到的

东西。

提到创新教育，魏丹女士表示，应该将培养出色人才作为大学的使命。现今，大学并不是唯一可以学到知识的地方，但大学是塑造人格的地方。教师不仅为学生指引方向，更要教导他们方法与技巧。教师最终的目标是学生能够超越自己。只有教导出出色的学生，一名教师才算完成了自己的使命。同时，教师起到的作用不仅仅是教导学生，还要作为学生的朋友并对其起到促进作用。年轻人更具备潜力，但同时也更易受挫，所以教师应当耐心关怀，鼓励学生一路向前。

最后，魏丹女士指出，当人们谈到在国际组织和公司工作的人才时，多数人想到的是高学历、专业知识和外语能力。这三点固然重要，但是更重要的是他们有正直与高尚的人格、有视野、有激情以及有不惧风险的精神。而为了使中国能在国际化的道路上越走越远，中国的大学应当以培养出这样的人才为目标。

CHAPTER 12

Ms. Kathleen Reddy Smith

玛瑞埃塔学院

Leader-in-Residence at Marietta College

"Be a Leader: Think Sharp and Write Brief"

Good morning, I was so honored to accept this position for which I have had the unwavering support of president and dean. I am grateful to them.

When he first asked me to be the leader in residence, he said, "how would you teach our students to be leaders?"

I replied that I had a theory that had worked over and over in both the private and public sectors and I wanted to teach that theory: be a leader: think sharp and write brief.

I believe that everyone including the most junior employees can lead or influence an organization when his junior rank means he is operating beneath the power curve if he thinks sharp and write brief.

How would I teach my students to think sharp and write brief and then to use those skills to lead or to influence? I would teach in the following way: build their strategic analytic skills so they would precisely identify a problem; define those strategic analytic skills even further to identify which facts are crucial and which are not; to teach students to write so clearly and briefly as to capture even the attempt of a busy decision.

First, my teaching revolutionized how students think and write. I was for them like putting their right shoe on the left foot and putting their left shoe on their right foot.

Why was it so awkward? I wanted them to write for busy decision makers, to get the attention of CEO, the senior partner in the law firm, the foreign minister by making the text very short with recommended decision up front to catch their decision makers' attention. This approach contradicted what the academic world required. Professors expect long paper full of footnotes to prove the student has researched his topic well. Here was my second challenge: there is a lot of information out there, how does a student decide what is relevant? The answer is to use strategic analysis to separate fact from fiction, separate fact from opinion and separate relevant from irrelevant and keep doing it again and again like practicing the scales on a piano. In other words, you learn strategic analysis by doing it again and again. That process of identifying relevant facts is complicated in today's world where there is too much information.

A French filmmaker predicted 20 years ago that the world would be awash in information and isn't that so with the Internet and 24-hour news?

We will no longer travel. It will no longer be necessary to travel with television when you need eight days to travel around the world. So she says that what is important is not all the answers readily available at the click of a mouse, not all answers but the correct answer to correct question.

This is where the practical value of strategic analysis is. If you have so much information, what information is essential to making a particular decision? This is what I wanted to do, to have students prepare for a successful professional life and suggest a solution so he could ignore the problem and consider the excellent solution.

Let's begin by discussing the importance of strategic analysis to define the problem and find the best solution.

First let's talk about defining the problem. In 1970s, the architectural firm in London built a skyscraper for the sole use of one law firm. To hold down the land cost, they built it thin and high and economized further on the number of elevators. They calculated the number of elevators needed by concluding that an employee would use the elevators twice a day. But they did not factor that employees need to use it to go to meetings during days. What architects do was that they did not have interior space to add another elevator nor could they install an elevator on the exterior. So they probed further and asked more questions. It turned out that the employees did not feel inconvenienced but rather were bored waiting. Then they installed floor-to-ceiling mirrors in hallways where the elevators opened on each floor. The mirrors permitted employees who were waiting for the elevators an opportunity to look at themselves. The employees' charges of being inconvenienced vanished.

The lesson is that sometimes the problem as stated is not the problem. And you have to find what the exact problem is. The real problem is the boring employees. And the answer was the mirrors would help.

The importance of strategic analysis to another lesson is to find the best solution to a problem.

I begin to say that some blind people love to play golf. The sighted golfers asked the golf course management to ban the blind. Management thought the problem was due to a lack of empathy for the other. They thus called in a minster to press both to understand the position of the other side. But the golfers who could see did not budge; they wanted the blind be banned from the course.

Next, management thought the problem might be a medical one. The doctor said there was no such device.

Finally, management contacted an engineer and "This is easy." the engineer said. They extended the time the golf course was open and so they played at night and freed the golf course. So, strategic analysis can lead us to the optimum solution.

Everyone, even the most junior employee, can lead or influence an organization, if s/he thinks sharp and writes brief. How did I teach students to think sharp and write brief? I built their strategic analytic skills to enable them to precisely identify a problem. I developed those strategic analytic skills further to identify which facts are critical, and which are not, to solving a problem. I taught students to write so clearly and so briefly as to capture even the attention of a busy decision maker in their first professional position after college.

Two challenges to get students to accept the "Think Sharp/Write Brief" Approach. First challenge: my teaching revolutionized how students think and write. First, I required students to make the text very short when professors would require them to write a long text full of footnotes to show mastery of the subject. Second, I instructed students to put the issue for decision at the start—a device to get the decision maker—the CEO, the foreign minister, the partner in the law firm—to focus immediately on the problem and the suggested solution.

Second challenge: there is a lot of information, everywhere. How do you decide what is relevant? Answer: strategic analysis. You learn strategic analysis by doing it again and again. As the Greek philosopher Aristotle once said, "Excellence is not an act, but a habit."

In summary: in the end, what is more important is not all the answers readily available on the Internet, but the correct answer to the correct question.

Let's do some strategic analysis. Process of judging the true value of statements: what information is essential to making a particular decision? Is the source of that information reputable? Is one fact more important than another? Can we accept a fact from a third-hand source, or should we only rely upon a primary source? Is a fact really a fact, or is it an opinion? Can we make a decision based on opinion, or do we need to stick with just the facts? Strategic analysis is important to TWO critical processes: defining the problem and finding the best solution. Defining the problem: sometimes the problem as stated is not the problem. You must use strategic thinking to find the exact problem in order to find the right solution. Finding the best solution to a problem: you can use strategic analysis to find the best solution to a problem.

The LIR Project:

Description of my course at Marietta College: teaching partner: Dr. Mark Schaefer, Political Science Department Chair. Writing material: the 1979 Iranian Revolution. First text: Harvard case study entitled "Fall of the Shah of Iran." The second text: All Fall Down, by Gary Sick, White House Aide for Iran.

Description of my course at Marietta College: in college, a student writes long papers, full of footnotes, to demonstrate mastery of the topic. But in professional life, the new employee must immediately write briefly and precisely. How did I begin to teach professional writing?

Step One: Review of English Grammar and Composition No one can write well if they do not understand grammar and how to write basic text. So, I first reviewed English grammar and composition, beginning with how to construct a sentence and then a paragraph. The approach is instructive and fun. And strategic analytic skills are to define the policy problem and then to suggest a workable solution. In case of me, I like to remind people of the very personalized education we give. While the professor guided our students through the strategic analysis of the decision making, I began the professional writing class.

Step Two: One-Page Synopsis (or Summary)

I then taught our students how to write a one-page synopsis of a much longer text. This process used Professor Schaefer's strategic analysis lessons—forcing students to decide which facts to eliminate in the one-page synopsis but still convey the longer text's substance. I told students to write the paper as if they were working and had to brief their boss. "Think sharp/write brief," I said.

Step Three: Turning a One-Page Summary into a Briefing Memorandum for a Boss.

I then built on this exercise—writing a one-page synopsis—to show them how to write a briefing paper for their boss. I introduced the concept of "clearing" their paper in the large organization where they worked. The CLEARANCE PROCESS ensures the briefing paper that goes to everyone's boss has the wide "clearance", or buy-in or support of other colleagues working the same issue and that the decision maker (boss) has the best possible advice to make the best decision.

Step Four: Boiling Facts Down to Write Press Guidance I also taught students how to write press guidance. Use one paragraph of background and talking points. Again, students must understand the very essence of a subject.

Step Five: Boiling Facts down Even More to write a "Pull-aside" What is a pull-aside, you ask? There are times in life when you serve as the principal staffer to an important person. World events move fast. Sometimes you must convey in the briefest way possible news of a late-breaking event to your principal.

There is a famous saying of Aristotle "Excellence is not an act, but a habit." And I would add, strategic analysis can be taught and practiced again and again till perfect. Even the most junior employee can influence or lead an organization through good strategic analysis and writing skills. One way to lead/influence the organization is through a "decision memorandum." A decision memorandum is brief to encourage a busy decision maker to read it. It includes only facts necessary to make the decision. It puts the decision that must be made as the first paragraph. With this skill, an employee can influence/lead the organization even from below the power curve. In my experience, the employee who masters this skill can lead the organization from below the power curve. I am putting on the screen now an example of decision memorandum done by one of our students. The issue for decision was whether the United State should permit a visa to enter.

We have a second-semester program which mainly goes like this: we assigned each student a particular country to research—Belgium, Indonesia, etc. To encourage strategic analytic skills, we had students determine the U.S. national interest in that country. After they wrote a series of three papers, we traveled to Washington, D.C. In Washington, we scheduled their final oral exams with officers in the U.S. Foreign Service, our diplomatic corps. We arranged a tour to the State Department Operations Center. We visited the Barbados Embassy, where a Marietta College graduate, John Beale, is Barbados Ambassador to the United States. We also have a Capstone to the Washington visit: the Bacon House. Why did we meet at the Bacon House? The Capstone to the Washington visit was a luncheon at the historic Bacon House, the home of an organization of foreign affairs professionals, one block from the White House. I wanted to showcase our great students and to thank my colleagues for helping with exams. The house was grand and welcoming, and full of art. I wanted our students to see this, because it symbolizes the graciousness of diplomatic life. But I also wanted them to see the reality—that life as a diplomat can be hard and dangerous, too.

I then brought the discussion of Iran from fall semester, back full-circle. The speakers are two Iran hostages, Michael Merino, held in solitary confinement for most of 444 days in 1979, and Ambassador Bruce Lange. They were powerful symbols of the demands of public service—and what it takes to be a leader when your life is in danger. Marietta College excels at experiential learning, which is learning by immersion in an experience. Unlike internships where a student can flounder with no guidance, Marietta's experiential learning is done in tandem with a professor or leader-in-residence or executive-in-residence. This approach allows a student to be independent, but retains access to a professor or the McDonough Leadership Center for help, as necessary.

Strategic analysis prepares you for life and to live life to its fullest. Then it was historic visit of Minneapolis Orchestra to Havana. After the performance, the musicians repaired to a Cuban nightclub. The woman is a bassist from Minneapolis and the man, a Cuban musician or nightclub patron. They' ve danced before, though not with one another. They needed to figure out which way the other person was going. It' s a perfect example of strategic analysis.

Based on their earlier experiences of dancing and "figuring it out," they know exactly where to look for direction.

I would like to end with the photograph of the historic visit. After the performance, the musicians repaired to a Cuban nightclub to listen to music. She is a bassist and a Cuban musician or a nightclub patron. So one imagines the music was so compelling that both these people found each other to dance. But as strangers, they needed to figure out which direction the other person was going. In a perfect example, they know exactly where they look.

They look at each other' s feet. You know they have danced before though not with one another. Despite their lack of familiarity with one another, they know exactly where to look for direction and where to go on next, based on their earlier experiences of figuring it out. In short, they are calling upon their strategic analytic skills and as usual, art, the art of the dance says it better than I could: when you don' t know exactly where to go. Use strategic analytic skills you have practiced time and again to solve the newest problem of where to go next.

Thank you very much. I am happy to take any questions about my role as leader-in-residence at Marietta College.

摘要

"成为领导者:敏锐思考和简洁表达"

Kathleen Reddy Smith 玛瑞埃塔学院

Kathleen Smith 女士介绍了自己对学生思维方式和表达能力进行革新的方法,让学生学会"敏锐思考和简洁表达"。该过程中需要克服两个挑战:一是在教学过程中转变学生的思考和写作方式。Smith 的做法是:要求学生用简洁的文字进行书面表述,这与完成教授的学术论文要求有所不同。其次,她指示学生在一开始就针对问题给出初步策略,即针对问题和建议的解决方案,供决策者(首席执行官、外交部长、律师事务所合伙人)参考。

第二个挑战是面对大量无处不在的信息,如何确定真正相关的内容。答案是战略分析, 反复进行分析,一步一步确认完成。Smith 女士提到了古希腊哲学家亚里士多德说过的一句话:优秀不是一种行为,而是一种习惯。

但更重要的并不是能轻易从互联网上得到的答案,而是需要针对正确的问题给出正确的答 案。

随后,Smith 女士以判断语句价值为例,就战略分析过程进行了简单讲解:要判断哪些是对做出具体决定必不可少的信息;信息来源的可信度是否也是判断标准之一;如何判断多个事实的重要性;是接受来自第三方来源的事实,还是应该只依赖一个主要来源;某些情况下所谓的"事实"究竟是事实还是看法;决策过程中是否可以参考观点,还是只能参考事实。

最后,Smith 女士指出,战略分析包括两个关键过程:定义问题和找到最佳解决方案。定义问题,要使用战略思维来寻找确切的问题;而寻找最佳解决方案则需要使用战略分析。

CHAPTER 13

Mr. Ulrike Reisach

新乌尔姆应用技术大学

Neu-Ulm FH：Fachhochschule Neu-Ulm

Stimulating Creativity and Innovation through Education in Applied Sciences

Thank you. So welcome everybody, I'm very happy to see so many people here, I was wondering whether they come for me or for Andy, it is a careful thought that he's from Harvard. Andy, you have it good because whatever you say, as you are from Harvard, must be true and must be excellent. Or they will come for big concert that follows afterwards. So I think all of the reasons are combined, and we got up early but we are fresh. And where I will start right now is today's topic about simulating creativity and innovation. And since I come from a university of applied science which is a special type of universities in Germany, I thought I will tell you what we are doing there and how education there works and what it means. So let me glance into today's university's situation in China. As you see here, and this is an OECD report, so this is not my invention, this is by OECD, China has a very big university system with many graduates, but the problem is the graduates sometimes can't use their knowledge they acquired in the university properly. It really was not so much knowledge that they acquired, they got more information. So maybe it's the difference between applied things they have learned and just memorizing a lot of facts, a lot of theories and then putting them into practice. This is what they call the applicability of the knowledge and this seems to be a crucial point. You may reason for this that Chinese universities are very strongly exam-focused. I mean this has some tradition in the Confucius system which was all about passing the exams and making your careers, one step after the other, which is very nice. But since Confucius time until now, the challenges of reality have changed, so you need a little bit more than the pure accumulation of information. So this is why China now is trying to encourage creativity also, because the next step of Chinese industrialization process will definitely be that China has to go more innovative and has to conquer world markets with products that no one else ever has sold off. So this is the key to do so. Now I want again to ask you the difference between the information and knowledge and how those are gained and transformed in universities and elsewhere also in practical life. I mean never stop learning, you will learn every second of your life, and therefore you can't focus on your study in school only. Now I would go on to some basis of communication and the right media and right ways of transforming knowledge. Now I'll go to some inter-cultural aspects, because this is crucial for the learning process. And then I will point out the significance of the right way of communication for acquired knowledge and conclude with education of applied sciences and give some practical examples. So you see that is European way of doing things, doing it in a very structured way. And we put this in advance that you know exactly what is to be expected. Now here is the difference between information and knowledge. So you need to be able to decipher this kind of data to interpret it in order to be able to perform. So the two ladies you see, one of them, the upper one is my daughter with her harp, the other one is a Chinese artist which I photographed in Hangzhou. So similar the instruments they have, but they both need a deep practice, continuous practice, in order to be able to do this. Now knowledge means the ability to transform information into something unique. As you know, a good artist, a good musician, does more than simply playing like computer, a computer or anything could maybe also play the notes, but it would not sound convincing, it would not have any kind of empathy or it would not have the melody you want to hear from a good orchestra. So a good artist interprets the information gained and puts it into something unique, something that has not been done before, a performance that is very special. So in an office you also make sure to play along, nicely and have harmony. And if the artist is excellent, he or she may further develop the whole piece and not only stick to what one composer composed 200 years ago, but also develop and compose his own new sound. And this is what we call creativity. This is what we call innovation. You need not only to memorize what is given, you need also to practice what is put in front of you, you need to think further, and to practice further and develop new things. And this is where we are trying to enable you and trying to make you fit for a future that goes beyond the past. This is because we have set this, the student has somehow to be better than his master in the end. Well you should be better than Mozart and Beethoven, if you are a good musician, so this means you have to try to be better than many others and to compose new things. And even it's more than music, it doesn't matter. Maybe the time has changed and maybe the taste and expectations are different now. Now let us see how this is done. Normally the learning thing as understood in many universities many years ago was you have the data, you have the information and you give the information to the students and you hope this will end up in knowledge and good practice. But I put a question mark here, because that is not so clear. We get the information but we are not 100% sure whether they will end up in knowledge. So therefore we should go a different way. The some curiosities and we know the student experience it themselves. Curiosity means that they have the opportunity to try it out. To see whether this could maybe work, also make some mistakes from a learning view, and then get to arise inside here. So knowledge also means selecting from much information. We want you to think the information clue and construct it in a new way. And this is how you create new knowledge, because you have thought it through, you go deeper and deeper into the core subject. And if you properly understand it, you do exactly know and put it together in a new and very concise way. And if you have learned how to do this, then you have really understood it. You don't just copy the given thing, if you understand it and formulate it in a way that you can understand and you can also give it to others. And also the sense-making process of learning so you see a certain sound in those things, you know what their purpose is, and if you know the purpose, this helps you to develop it further because in a few things when the purpose is not met 100% but 90% , you can do the rest 10% . Then that is going to sound making, so it gets from data to information, whose own sound making. We understand it and we understand the significance. Let's go to the next learning group, if we know the context, so when will this be applied, what could be the right opportunity to use this. This is where we gain knowledge. We also know about the conditions, about the expectations, and what experience others have made of it. If we gain that knowledge, we need additional motivation. So action never happens about motivation. So much of the knowledge acquired in our studies turns out not to be in this book. And we forget it. All we find boring we also forget it. So we need the motivation to really apply it, and the will to change something in the world. To make the world somewhat a better place to whatever actions you can do to rest on whatever opportunity. So this is the motivation, and you can operate and result in products you may come across. So the next step is competence. You need not ask someone, "May I do this? How do I do this? Can you tell me exact steps? Please tell me how to do this." This is not what you need. We need people who can do this from the beginning to a purpose for end. So this means the ability to think and act by yourselves. So this leads you to decision making, and also the capability of judgment. So it is usually value-based because you want to reach the purpose and, for example, values in society we discussed yesterday. And this enables you to make a decision and you need to make this decision very fast. Why decide fast? Give an example here. To make the right decision fast enough and that saves 150 people's lives. This is Soling Burger, the pilot of airplane A420 who encountered a bird swan close to New York City and the pilot immediately noticed he had to do something. So he couldn't ask anyone, he could not read handbooks at this every moment; he had to simply make a decision. This decision is "I have to do a water landing. Where can I do this in New York City?" He did this water landing and all people were saved. This was the right decision, and Burger is sixty plus something and he is not young, he has this experience gathered through his life as a pilot. He knows he is responsible for all people in the flying plane. So he made this decision and saved them. This is what we call leadership. You make right decision for yourself and all the people with you. So this is a one example of how to use the knowledge you have learned, and acquire through a lifelong experience. Now the different types of knowledge are often classified in a similar way and we can refer to the book Knowledge Transform and which was published two years ago. I work as a social psychologist, and there is much of knowledge in terminal logics. You learned a lot of definitions in your study courses, so this is the general knowledge. Public knowledge is collective, so that is the knowledge we acquire, in our history, more or less or mathematics before your life and the calculations you do. So this is all exquisite. There is another public knowledge which is the yellow here, which is more person related, person centered. This is the knowledge you have either gained from personal experience, for example if you know how to ride a bicycle, this is more toriconical knowledge. Also you know how to swim, so this is something you will probably never forget even if you haven't practiced for several years. This is your ability to do more conclusions to think logically and then you have intuitive knowledge, which is not so much ratio, but is more intuition. It has something to do with your stomach, your head; it's more in your assistance. And you may not be underestimated, because those are feelings that you are acquired even when you were a child. As a child, you know where the attention is in the room. You can guess when someone is happy or someone is unhappy. You need not think too much about it. You just got the empathy or the feeling and even a baby has this. So it also helps you sometimes decide which situation is dangerous and in which situation you can relax and take action or which direction we should go. So these are different types of knowledge, and it's difficult. We very often focus on this exquisite knowledge because this is what we can request, also our testing system of stimulation system. We have written exams, we only test the exquisite knowledge. We don't test whether students can do further judgment. We sometimes try by asking open questions. Open questions are a little bit better. Now what is this kind of knowledge? What does it comprise? What you see here is the knowledge based on the giving, is to know what, so it's the back of everything. The second thing is know how. So you need to know how you practice it, what kind of procedure you have to do. Know who is going to be forgotten, because very often in real life you cannot know all the details in every single problem. So you need to know who you are going to ask. Besides you need to know the same as to for company life. Then the companies are very often urgent so we need some suggestions for solving problems, and I ask "Who will run the company? Who is on this issue? whether this was an engineer, or the lawyer or for the stock change. And also I ask them, I interviewed them, and I was told what the issue was, and I asked the people what the pay was, maybe I formulated it to be too easy but this is the weight. And if they said yes, and this is what I could go over to the CEO, what the request for next step is. So this is why you need people because if you only look the organization of chart, and see Mr. and Mrs. who you never seen before, is responsible for this.

According to the organization on the chart in the phone book, you don't get what you want. You need a person who you trust and who knows you and who also provides you with personal information. Because if they trust in your official talk, this is not very helpful, so I often go to persons who know me and who I know, this is the point I want to get here. Can you please tell me openly what we will gain behind this; we want to understand their interest and what the sensitive spots are here. And the information could only be exchanged between people who know each other well enough to talk so. I guess the Chinese know it very well because contexts have exquisite information which should be exchanged to know what the next thing is. I want my students to understand why things are happening. Why someone wants this or that piece of information or action, what is the interest behind it if they just take this as a joke and do not know the question then that maybe not helpful, because maybe they are going to make a mistake. So as the students are disabled to see what is behind it, they sometimes dare to do this. My students sometimes convert tasks from medium-sized company. They say, "The boss wants me to do this or that." I want to make an example of a German company; they want to know the big competitor. I once have done a research on the competitor. Someone was assigned to figure out the questions, "Do you know what kind of market volume they have or what patterns of structure? My boss told me that he wanted to inquire for this company." I said, "You had better to do some research. And then you tell your boss, the company, this is really a good idea. Americans should acquire more medium-sized company." And I said, "Please you have to tell company your strategies were." But how can I? But you have to, because this will lead you up to a managerial position. If you don't trust this kind of task which is the silly task, you will always be redundant for them. Company will end this kind of strategy. So you have to tell them somehow this idea is not good or there is a chance or maybe it can facilitate the kind of corporation between the two companies. We think of the task you give and only then you can make good suggestions. So this is what you need to know about, you know why the interest is behind it, and you can negotiate newly, you not only take on something that you had, and you try to find out the interest behind. How this can be required for learning. So we help you here on the left side, the passive learning, and the passive learning sticks to facts and figures. This is what you find in the books. We go through sometimes in teaching and we use videos, so we show them videos which we find on the Internet. Another thing we can do is to steal it. We just tell the student a story and the story sticks better in people's minds than anything else. But you need to know the right story. That means you need to have some life experience so that you can tell stories. Sometimes if the lecturer is so young and he only knows the text knowledge, he can just talk about the textbook knowledge. But if you have some practically experience, then you can go from this experience and you can also tell histories. Histories lay examples; maybe sometimes simplify them to get it done in a short time for our students to work on. This is close to what we call active learning, which means we let our students work on their own research. This is how they learn how to differentiate what is essential from what is just nice to have. Very often they get lost in the overflow of information especially on the Internet. At times they will go as they have got, it's so much out there. And usually the topics are way too boring. The topics are as boring as this, annoying. And next time they talk about research question now I don't find the answer, no one has heard of this before. This is what science is, you are answering new questions, you are answering questions that no one before has answered. Because if they have already been answered by anyone, then why should you do it? Why do you repeat what someone else has said? So that is not your job, your job is always doing something new. Experience how you can get this practice inside. So when we frequently invite knowledgeable people from the companies to my university. I have similar people from local industries and colleagues and friends recently and we have people from business associations and we talk. This is how we get the practical knowledge and the universities and students like this, because they see "OK. It really meets what we learned; it's much like what our professors said but this is how the companies are doing in the daily business life." Next step will be monitoring and we are playing shadow. So we have an obligatory semester when our students will take internship. They are admitted for the bachelors before they have required in semester. So six months in a company. And they have to write reports about this thing, about this task, so this is not only working in an organization. We try to make sure this is substantial in the experience they got, so usually this is the fourth semester and students come back from their first semester and find much more mature personalities. They very often know why they are studying in this topic. Because they have seen what they have learned and what they saw in the company. So this is a step of first inversion that come of the jobs, they do what they call "gathered experience". So they have to do their job on their own, but there is still someone there that is a supervisor. The students have graduated; they work on their own but there could be s kind of coach who helps the person if they have any kind of question, so this is how you want to make this experience work in the future. There are some ways in universities that can bring in all kind of professions. Here is an example of medical professor, so medical doctor has to identify diseases according to the syndrome from a way, from what they get. If you haven't experienced it you won't see much. But if you've experienced this, then you can see some kind of crucial aspects. So the future medical doctor needs to exercise this. This seems to also apply to the situation when you help with a building plan. If you are in this business, you do immediately see what will work and what won't. And you do this now and they have to be experienced to be able to do this. Now, how does communication help this? First of all, we need a way of thinking, what steps back from the information given. Ask yourself if this is a good piece of information. Is this accurate?

Who has been adding this? Is the information balance or biased? Who is the author? I very often ask my students who you know you are and who is the Internet. Does the Internet take any responsibility? You know how much nonsense is on that. So therefore please, you can look deeper and find out where is the author from, is he or she a scholar? Does he or she present some interest for business or for politics or for political direction? There is something they have to find out, because they can better access what kind of sources they have. Very often they have different sources. So what should I think? I said this is usually from you who makes a list of criteria, which are important for the issue and then you decide which source is used for and how you make this useful source. You discuss the source aid, have this kind of background and be useful for these issues and be better for that. The source is not good at all because it is not so accurate. This is the task for the students. And this is the difficulty for them to see because they are not used to questioning sources so much. They sometimes think someone must be good. We have so much now on the Internet and so much on the newspaper you never find, so if you sometimes find it easier if there are reasons if there are evidence given, then this is a good. The author shows his/her personality by the works published, and the audience to whom he/she is addressing can tell in a scientific way. Audience is a significant school. And then last but not least, about sources, you need to switch to many scientific sources from like you know the globe that you can trust. If you use some site sources, I mean which is www, Home Burk by someone; I mean how you can cope with another student if that's not you. I know simply it's not good work. You see most of my highlights I took for I have this underline, I try to respect the copy right. Copy right issues too I had recently took away my students who delivered me a paper where I could tell by the language and then I gave to my assistant to put this to a checking system I got the percentage of 89%, I gave it back and told the Korean so and I was almost thinking why I should do this. But maybe you are not aware of this, so I will give you a second chance. I want you to redo this, I want your own thoughts, and I want everything but to take another thought grown properly. So they learned after the third attempts. This is sometimes difficult, but this is what we have to encourage them to do. Now make an academic approach to high-level sources. And the students sometimes do not know where the need is in our ordinary day. Neither has to be simple but accurate and has also in the neutral vocabulary. You do not blame anyone. You do not call anyone' s names or things to be as neutral as you can be as a researcher. Then you try to find connections and link to other topics and you draw conclusions and you try to convince your readers that what you have come to a conclusion is right. So it' s on arguments. This is also correction of ethics. So as a leader, you need to consider what I am doing. Do you do the thing for a good purpose and have you considered potential outcomes? This is what usually the famous German sociologists call consequentialism. So it is responsibility ethics. You are responsible for all your actions, what you are causing of them and what your interests behind it are, instead of trying to hide information away. So both things, the good intentions combine with good outcomes. This is what makes you responsible. And this is what you' ve got to consider. This is not easy sometime in decision making, because you do not know what the outcomes will be. No one of us knows the future. Yesterday we made a big picture of the future, but the problem is that this is more or less a fantasy. What we can do is that we can try to do in the path of analysis. So we can try to find out how our actions influence the outside world. This is where we get to know our goal, so everyone around us and we need to engage in sometimes discussion. And this is what will be the best way, especially if you are in a business which is a big global business, or if you are in a political world. Because in the political world, you have so many interests on you and you have to serve on them equally but sometimes miss out the important book and therefore you need to discuss this to get to know feeling of what would be fair and what can be decided with causing to anyone. So this is the decision making. You engage in this kind of state. You try to find out what are the principles of values, what are the considerations. You engage in the teaching planning for a looking planning or any business like this. If you want to be sustainable and have the success for twenty, thirty years, you need to do this for teaching then you try to exert great effort in those groups and discourse process. And the main purpose for this is you are learning. The outside world looks like your company and you have something to lose or win which is your reputation. If you make a mistake, they can only blame you if you never try to find this out, so as transparent communication. And I totally find common agendas and common goals and actions. Now you have formulated technical amounts of social responsibility. And this is really nice of you to share because they take co-active actions before required; many companies only react to play by the question. This is not good. So do it before you try to when solving problems, try to engage in environmental social programs if it is not legally required. Do this voluntarily. Do this out of your own responsibility without any society. And now also if something has happened, admit what has happened and correct it. And also some profits and good advice and this is beside it. And I think you have some enterprises that damage the environment, give them this list, and tell them this is good ethical behavior, and that could probably help it. Just one brief idea on that. We are all in the environment as you find here. But we have different thinking patterns, which are related to our languages and how we formulated thoughts. The values of the answers may be different. But sometimes our understanding of the words is different. Even though they are translated we don't understand the meanings of different ones. So we have the next levels of selected expectation of models which are different. Next level policy institution economy also the education system itself might be different. And they are close to what we find here, the groups and the families and the individuals. This is the pattern in need of all those expectations, and the individuals cannot change conditions so much, but together they can, because the expectations change in the society and we have seen lots of things that have changed in China since the last twenty or thirty years so you see all the individual can conduct different behavior then. Now give you a few examples on that. Terms like creativity, innovation, even science and practice might be differently interpreted in different cultures and then conditions. Authors like me in universities also go mad in institutional governmental organization. I work under different conditions to publish, and to think about things, about the societies. So the different levels of dependence and independence would be different. And we have to consider this. We may not transfer something from one culture to another and they should equally use this. So we can try to create awareness of those factors which will help us transform in a way appropriate. Now I want to give you an example here. Between the United States and China, the major differences, we have alphabet and that's how we write and think. We have lots of grammar. English is not so much like German which has much more grammar and has language like Latin and so on. So this makes us typical and logical thinkers. Since childhood, we have learned to compose a sentence logically. I also asked the "why" question way off, because in critical question you end up into the why. Why the ultimate reason ended up in the upper good? This is a period of why ends. China has a different language system. Its language does not have grammar in the sense we know it, the grammar is less precise. It is much more implicit because you can read between the lines and interpret the things and in very different manners. So sometimes for one Chinese sentence you can gain five different translations. Make a concise expression, you might get Chinese people into difficulties because concise and Chinese are incompatible. There is nothing concise. It's all interpreted. We often have the situation that we have a different context. You interpret the context well, the situation has changed. And Chinese do it and interpret it, the all thinkers as well, so there are much more possibilities in the thinking. So the main question is who it is, and what is it for. So they are two different questions. So who said it, which time, under which circumstance, and it's still appropriate now we have to change it. Very often the language has many things in piece that have benefit and long-term relationship. It is important to repeat it very often. So we say it is unconsciously, from the western point of view. But in Chinese's view, the relationship is of great meaning, they want to reach you at more harmony-related levels and for further dialogue. So what we see here is deductive thinking, so we have one idea, for example, the law, so we deduct, so it is very rational, whereas in young years, things are interurban. There is a piece of the dark side of the mountain and the sunny side of the mountain. There is a piece of the sunny side and the dark side and they are in the same mountain, but simply on different sides. So that is called "belong together". It is the unification of a part of abiotic. So this is the different concert of the world, which is good, because China has never been aggressive. They always see the thing in the harmonious way and they try to learn from others and do things in a harmonious way. And this is quite interesting for us. They could also say that they are reasoning; there are differences. We are more wood-face logical, influenced by logistical thinking, which is also mathematical thinking, words and intuitive thinking which holistic thinking in all aspect is. So, uh, I love this comparison because in Germany we have a lot of this, not the capitalism in the US systems and it is far from socialism. So what is it? We have a so-called social market economy, the economy with social elements. This not only came after the WWII, but long tradition thinking. What do you think about companies? So Americans very strongly focus on customers, competitors and their investors. This is what they do in the whole company business thing. Germany much more focuses on the employees. We do not ask what kind of company. We first ask how many employees you have, which means job creation. For us job creation is more important. And also do you pay taxes? How about a society? Do you have a societal engagement? Do you save the environment? So those are the questions we ask and media has a high role. So it is a different approach. And also in terms of leadership, they focus on the business more. As sales persons, they are marketing themselves and businesses; this is where we can learn from. We have traditional craftsman who love the products, they will never change the company's purpose even though they could make more money, because they are production-focused and technology-focused. And they have a profession which is life-long profession. They don't have so many frequent changes; they also have high continuity and quality efforts. There are different leadership models behind this, and in the western world we have the kind of manager models. Model No. 1, we see leaders as coaches who try to put the outside of the way and enable people to go their way on their own. Model No. 2 is they can see from China, we are the manager who defines the goals and the way to reach it. This is what experience chines interns and they often ask me how do you want it. Sometimes I don't know exactly how I want it, I want the suggestion, but they will not prepare to do this because they do not dare to make me as their boss. But this is a problem: very often the bosses need suggestions from someone else in order to make a decision, so in a case here is that on the Model No. 1, the employee can succeed as well, we want employees who have international thinking and make suggestions. Therefore we have acquirement for international management and related competency, social competency, and some kind of self-competency. So you think about yourself, your own actions and how can you make it better. This is curiosity. Curiosity is a good thing; it feeds up learning, and also some sensitivity, which we try to turn them to also international exchange, experience of what, and experience of colleagues or co-students from other class. So we often try to select the employees who have competencies which means we go into centers so they can be false. They can be related to the subject, but the assessment put them in a situation: it's a company situation, simulated and to provide some kind of suggestions. So this is really difficult but this is really what we see in candidates who can apply the knowledge. And this applied knowledge is where I want to move here, who come to this session innovation, it' s not only technical. Their all access can be organizational, like Amazon, Amazon never invented a product. It invented a business model, and it can be societal innovation. Like for example, product which are renewable and economical and healthy products. So for a feeling to this means they are showing what they care. I don' t know whether the energy they gain weighs much but it is a signal which they are sending now one question to you: what makes you creative. If you want to be creative in the university, if you want to have some good ideas for your chart, what could be the in condition? One thing is motivation, to have the courage to try. Maybe you don' t know but you have freedom to try. This is one point, you need this kind of reader and if you make a mistake, you are not punished. There is no silly question; there is only silly answer (student' s answer). She thinks from different aspects. This is why we are here, we get different personalities, we also try to encourage you to see the world in different pieces. This is why we are here. There is one more important thing, diversity of opinions, and also culture of dialogue. And why I show you pictures? Just to inspire you. This is in one of the big mechanical companies in Germany. Mechanical companies generally have bad image while this one has a good image. Try to resemble this in the corporate architecture. My colleagues and my learning campus, they have this kind of place where people can sit down and rest and have some inspiring thoughts. So this is just an idea for you, there are a lot more, for example the freedom, you develop the process to decide what you really want to have in the profession, what you want to do next. So, there are many different ways to develop your own personal career and go into profession. There is a Chinese proverb but I can only know the Latin proverb: the purpose of learning is not just going into university, the purpose is applying it. So you try to apply it and we try to teach you. Application does not mean stupid type. This is something that so many young people spending their whole life on. What we want to teach you is thinking further and this also means critical thinking and selecting your own method, and also digging deeper into complexity, so it helps in critical thinking and for entrepreneurs in grasping opportunities. This is what we need and this is something we need to create and try. You try this by letting it go and so choose but normally we just speak and act on your own. That means you are engaged in simulations and gains that you have to train like a pilot. And simulator and some simulated you to learn how to make decisions, and you end up in international experience management, and this is what I was in my university. Einstein was born here, Einstein was a scientist but the same time a thinker, so he had things sometimes the public acting more like the thinker. So this is somewhat funny but this is typical creative mind. And this is also inspired. This is nearly one for the excellent because it is the best location, because everyone wanted to come though simply good. So you need more and just lead a life you want as well.

推动应用科技教育的创新性与创造力

UlrikeReisach　新乌尔姆应用技术大学

UlrikeReisach 教授的演讲以分析中国大学教育特点为切入点，指出当今中国大学毕业生普遍存在无法将自身所学应用到实际工作中的现象。其原因在于自古以来，中国的教育体系将考试摆在极其重要的位置，导致学生学习倾向于记忆既有事实和理论，而这只是信息摄入的过程。她认为知识不同于信息，是一种将信息转化、细分、整合进而创造出新事物的能力。其中，基于自身实际经历的思考是必不可少的环节。如今，人才应当掌握的是知识，而不仅仅是信息。之后，Reisach 教授分享了自己在德国的教学经验：首先学生学习的动力来源于对知识的应用，应用知识的过程可以激励学生对知识的理解与思考,进而催生创新。其次在教学过程中应当引导学生从以下几个方面对已有案例进行思考:第一,要清晰地了解事实内容;第二,要明白如何用它来指导实际;第三,要找到一位彼此相互了解并且可以答疑解惑的导师;最后,要思考为什么会发生这样的事情,主人公做出这样的决定的动机是什么。此外,在德国会采用两种方法让学生在应用的过程中掌握知识、思考创新:首先将具有丰富工作经验的人士请进课堂,与学生交流自己的经历与体会;其次为学生安排为期六个月的实习机会,并撰写总结报告,让学生在实际应用中完成对知识的巩固与思考。